Suffolk
County Council

Please return/renew this item
by the last date shown.

Suffolk Libraries
01473 584563
www.suffolk.gov.uk/libraries/

Wealth Journey™

9 Steps to a Wealthier You

Kiki Theo

PENGUIN BOOKS

PENGUIN BOOKS

Published by the Penguin Group
Penguin Books (South Africa) (Pty) Ltd, 24 Sturdee Avenue, Rosebank,
Johannesburg 2196, South Africa
Penguin Group (USA) Inc, 375 Hudson Street, New York, New York 10014, USA
Penguin Group (Canada), 90 Eglinton Avenue East, Suite 700, Toronto, Ontario,
Canada M4P 2Y3 (a division of Pearson Penguin Canada Inc)
Penguin Books Ltd, 80 Strand, London WC2R 0RL, England
Penguin Ireland, 25 St Stephen's Green, Dublin 2, Ireland (a division of Penguin
Books Ltd)
Penguin Group (Australia), 250 Camberwell Road, Camberwell, Victoria 3124,
Australia (a division of Pearson Australia Group Pty Ltd)
Penguin Books India Pvt Ltd, 11 Community Centre, Panchsheel Park, New Delhi
– 110 017, India
Penguin Group (NZ), 67 Apollo Drive, Mairangi Bay, Auckland 1310, New Zealand
(a division of Pearson New Zealand Ltd)

Penguin Books (South Africa) (Pty) Ltd, Registered Offices:
24 Sturdee Avenue, Rosebank, Johannesburg 2196, South Africa

www.penguinbooks.co.za

First published by Penguin Books (South Africa) (Pty) Ltd 2010

Copyright © Kyriaki Theodosiadis 2010

ISBN 978 0 143 02674 7

Typeset by Nix Design in 11.2/14.2 pt Revival 555
Cover by Minette de Villiers
Printed and bound by Interpak Books, Pietermartizburg

Acknowledgement
The quotation from *Mental Fight* by Ben Okri is reproduced by kind permission of
Orion Publishers

This book is not intended to provide personalised legal, accounting, financial, or
investment advice. Readers are encouraged to consult competent professionals with
regard to matters such as interpretation of law, proper accounting procedures, financial
planning and investment strategies. The author and the publisher specifically disclaim
any liability, loss or risk which is incurred in consequence directly or indirectly, of the
use and application of any contents of this work. The author of this book does not
dispense medical advice or prescribe the use of any technique as a form of treatment
for physical or medical or emotional problems without the advice of a doctor, either
directly or indirectly. The intent of the author is only to offer information of a general
nature to help you on your quest for emotional and spiritual well-being.

For Shaun, Alex and Sasha

And at first we will seem adrift
On a strange sea where fishes
No longer resemble what they used to be,
And where we are no longer
What we were,
Or thought we were.

And we will have become less,
Or more,
Depending on what we have
Brought with us
From the old time,
The old space.

Ben Okri, from *Mental Fight*

Contents

1. WHERE YOU ARE

2. WHERE YOU ARE GOING

5.   WHY YOU ARE STILL NOT THERE   191

6.   WHAT TO DO ONCE YOU GET THERE   227

INTRODUCTION

Let the Wealth Journey Begin

Most of the details of this book are contained in the chapter headings and descriptions. If you were simply to contemplate each line, as well as its interaction with the other lines and sections, you would have the gist of the book. But perhaps you would not feel inclined to buy a book with just four pages in it ...

For the rest, this is quite a zippy book. With so many sections, it has to be. And it's about money and the money-making journey. Follow the guidelines and you will get there, far quicker than you thought. Don't get caught up in huge 'meaningfulness' or seriousness, treat it like a holiday. This is a Wealth Journey™ for everyone and anyone, no matter where you are in your wealth programme. Keep it short and light, like the chapters. Be curious to discover new terrain.

Approach challenges like a knight on a quest – armed with your magical sword and a brave heart – even if you are a girl! Retrace your steps back from a wealth detour and get on track. Don't waste time trying to figure out the whys of the detour, just get back on track.

Why all the 9s you may ask? Well, 9 is the number of completion. It is the greatest of all primary numbers because it contains all the qualities of all the others. It is the number of consciousness. It represents the 8 steps around the cycle of life plus the still centre.

This is what the Wealth Journey™ ultimately represents. It is our journey of transformation of self, through the various levels of consciousness and self-expression until we can feel the connection with the still point in the centre of our being.

Our connection with the centre, with the divine spark within, with the creative light that illuminates us, is, and always has been there. It may become obscured from time to time by illusion, or we may forget that we are the source of this light and not the lanterns on the side of the road of our travels.

This book is a reminder to us all that we are both the creators and the travellers of all our journeys. We are the light that illuminates our path. We are the goal we aspire to attain. We are the wealth we try to acquire.

But until we rediscover these profound truths ... we may as well go for the cash! If you are laughing, this is not a joke (but keep it up!). If you are not laughing, then it is – so lighten up!

It is my intent that reading this book will lead you to your highest truth, and expand your wealth in every way! May your path be paved with gold. It is my intent to sell millions and millions of copies of every one of my books around the globe. I dedicate the merit of this work to our enlightenment and the enlightenment of all beings.

Kiki Theo, March 2010

The Wealth Journey™

How to use this book

1. To derive maximum benefit from this book, state your specific intent for what you want to achieve at the start of the book and before each reflection.
2. Do the reflections lightly, with attention and the right intent.
3. When you free write allow undiscovered aspects of yourself and the subject you are exploring to emerge without censorship. Write to discover what you may not be conscious of.
4. When you are connecting with or discovering the feeling that corresponds to a particular consciousness level or level of self-expression, allow the emotion to arise without judgement, and simply experience it.
5. Perform inspired actions with intent, and use your will and focus to honour any commitment made in the various exercises.
6. Trust the process. Trust that it will produce the results you want.
7. Above all else, have fun!

The Basic Assumptions

The basic assumptions in this book are:
- Everything is energy
- Everything is connected
- How you do anything is how you do everything

For really in-depth discussion on these topics you need to read my other books. Here we will touch on these assumptions since they form the pillars for this work, and provide an explanation (of sorts) for the creative type tools we use.

If you think about it for a moment, the second two assumptions arise out of the first.

Because everything is energy, everything is connected. Because everything is connected, how you do anything is how you do everything. And because this is so, when you change one thing in your life, everything changes. In particular, when you change (or initiate) an action in full consciousness, with focused intent – say, on increasing your wealth – then not only does everything change, but the new impetus created becomes channelled and directed towards your intent, i.e. the creation of wealth.

Put your attention now on the fact that everything is energy, that everything is connected, and that therefore when you change one thing, everything else changes too. Put your focus and intent on changing aspects of yourself thereby changing your wealth profile!

Working with Reflection

Throughout this book you are asked to reflect on a number of questions which are posed at the end of each chapter. These questions are aimed at creating a shift in the way you see the world. They will help you discover deeper layers of yourself, as well as the way you approach and feel about the various aspects of the Wealth Journey. Do not ignore or skip the reflections, but also do not allow not doing them to stop you from reading further. Continue to read, but do come back to the reflections later, as they will help with your transformation and your journey.

Reflecting is allowing both the question and your answers to it to wash over you. You just observe what comes up. You look at what is there with an open and enquiring attitude, ready to discover something new, ready to be surprised. Whereas analysing is an event – it happens here and now, straight away – reflection is a process, and takes place over time. Allow time for the new to emerge. As you work though the chapters, your Wealth Journey will unfold – allow and embrace this journey.

Free writing

In the section on the 9 Wealth Challenges, you are asked to reflect through free writing – though you are most welcome (if not encouraged) to do the same throughout the rest of the book where you are simply asked to reflect.

Free writing is writing by allowing whatever emerges to emerge on the pages. You do not think about what to write, how to phrase it, or worry about grammar or punctuation. You merely allow your hand to write. The purpose behind all the writing is to discover the unknown, or the less obvious. Gently remind yourself of this purpose before you begin to write, though.

Summarising into one sentence at the end of an exercise after highlighting the most important parts may at first appear daunting, but it can be done. You are trying to get to the essence of what you are writing about. The summary does not need to be a logical conclusion derived from the sum total of your input. The summary is more a matter of asking yourself 'so what does all that really mean?' or 'what is at the heart of all I wrote?' Again, allow the summary to surprise you.

Summarising in this way is also practice for honing your focus and intent. To create what you want you need to get specific, and you need to get to the point. Summarising practice helps you to do just that.

When doing the writing exercises:

- Write for the recommended time only – use a timer
- Keep the pen moving, just write, don't think
- Do not censor anything – you can burn the paper later
- Begin with the prompt; if you become stuck, repeat the prompt

Working with image or symbol

A symbol is that which represents something by virtue of association, thought, or similar qualities. A symbol is not the same as a sign, which is a literal representation. For example, white, lion, cross are symbols of purity, courage, Christianity. They are universal, Western symbols. But symbol is also something very personal, different for everyone.

Words are the language of the rational and represent a certain type of thinking which is analytical, logical and realistic (unless you are free writing, that is). Symbol on the other hand is the language of a more creative type of thinking, intuitive, holistic, and deeply personal. When we integrate and align the two, we have much more creative potential at our disposal, much more energy and power.

Symbol, and its use in image work, is useful in expanding our perspective on life. Through skilful use of image work deep transformation of self and subsequently the world around us is made possible.

Through the use of image as symbol we can discover our innermost dreams and the means through which to attain them.

In the section on the 9 Dimensions of Self-Expression you are invited to create an image or symbol for each dimension, thereby expanding your perception and uncovering deeply rooted, and possibly unknown desires.

Allow whatever image comes to mind to exist without question. Do not dismiss the image because you may not like it, or because it may make no rational sense. Simply allow it to be. Reflect upon it, let it 'speak to you', and discover what you did not know before.

Inspired Decisions, Commitments and Actions

Do not become frightened by these very serious words. Throughout the book, at the end of each chapter, you are invited to translate and ground your realisations and reflections in decision and action. Once again, this may not necessarily be a logical or rational 'conclusion'. You may, for example, while reflecting on 'how to face money', decide you need to stand up to your bossy friend who keeps trying to set you up on a date, and say 'no'.

Everything is connected. Everything is linked. The important thing is to follow the instructions in this book, do as much of the work as is possible and comfortable for you at this time. Be gentle on yourself. You may decide, for example, that even though you know you need to reorganise your office, you are not ready to do so yet. That's fine. You can do it later.

But carry through, and once you commit, follow through on your commitments also.

You will also be asked, throughout this book, to initiate and cultivate activities that will enhance and support an increase and an expansion of wealth beingness. This is important. To change, you need to change – what you do, what you think, how you behave. These changes start with small, seemingly insignificant, successful and inspiring actions that need to be repeated over and over again until they become habit. Perform the actions.

Change, Change, Change

Change is not always comfortable. You will need time and space to integrate the changes in thinking and being that this work will initiate. You may also need to make some difficult decisions, take some action that will benefit you, though it may be hard to execute. Honour your commitment to act where required, and do so. Focus, and maintain your focus and intent. Absorb and cultivate the feelings and actions that will help to take you to the next level.

The tools you will use

To do the work in this book you will need a large A4 Wealth Journey book that you can write in; a pen and a few coloured pencils; an egg timer, or other type of timing device. Also:

- No logic, seriousness, or drawing of conclusions
- No correction, censoring, or holding back

- No one to ever look at what you have written, ever (unless you want it)
- A desire to change
- An open mind
- The readiness and willingness to fly!

The Power of Emotion

I have left the two most important things till last – emotion and intent. At almost every single exercise and point of reflection, action, commitment or focus, you are invited to connect with a feeling. That instruction is definitely not to be ignored. Our emotions are what lead us up the Wealth Consciousness scale. Emotion is what motivates and keeps the Wealth Journey going. When we seek wealth we are actually seeking the way the wealth will make us feel. Connecting with those feelings, recognising and understanding what they are, what they are connected to, and how we can activate them at will, is a practice which this book will fine-tune, if you follow the instructions. Calling up and using the emotions you associate with wealth are the quickest way to achieve what you want. We are not taught how to connect with our feelings – in fact we may have even been discouraged from doing so. Here you are asked to feel, feel, *feel*. Find out what wealth feels like, and it will be yours. It's as simple as that!

The Value of Intent

The key to the reflections, free writing and inspired actions is intent. Before you start, *set your intent.*

An intent contains an implied commitment to, and a decision to act towards, and achieve a want or desire. An intent is an act of focus and application of will and action.

So before you start reading this book (as well as before you do any of the recommended exercises in the book), *set your intent.*

Do that now.

Why are you reading this book? What are you hoping to learn, achieve?

What would need to happen in your life for you to know this book has produced results?

Be specific. Write a list if you need to. Be specific. What do you want? And what do you really want? What do you need, right now? It may have little to do with money.

Narrow down your list to the three most important things. Then pick what draws you the most at the moment. It does not really matter what it is, or whether it is logical. Don't make this too important.

Be specific. Say 'I want . . . .'

Then state this as an intent.

Do this here . . . . I intend to . . . .

Do not create an intent out of negating something. Rephrase any negative want.

For example, instead of 'I intend to have no debt', make it 'I intend all my accounts to be in credit'. Don't make this big and heavy, or Very Important. Just create an intent which will act as a beacon and goal, helping you gain maximum benefit from reading this book.

How much benefit you receive from your reading, how great a shift takes place in your life, how effortlessly you transform, how smoothly you increase your wealth, depends *on your decision* to do so.

Decide now that this is a life changing moment. Decide now that this is where your wealth makes a fast shift forward. Decide now that this is the book that will change everything! Are you ready?

If not, what do you need to do to be ready? What do you need to let go of? What do you need to say 'no' to? What do you need to say 'yes' to?

Decide to do it. Do it. Do whatever you need to do to become ready for your Wealth Journey.

Are you willing?

This is what real readiness is all about. Draw on your willingness to move forward and change. Draw on your willingness to go into the unknown and bring back the treasure.

Are you ready?

Alrighty then! (picture Jim Carrey here saying this ...)

The most important requirement for this work is a light touch. Keep it fun. Keep it magical. Keep focused on the light. And trust the process.

Let the Wealth Journey™ begin!

The Wealth Journey™

Let the Journey Begin

Your Wealth Journey began the day you were born. You brought wealth into someone's life – untold, immeasurable wealth. New life, what price can be put on that? The preciousness of human birth is a key reflection in Buddhism. It is said that human birth is as rare as a turtle swimming across all the oceans of the world, coming up for air every thousand years, putting her neck through a single hoop which is floating somewhere in the oceans. Imagine that!

Contemplating the preciousness of human birth is very useful, as it naturally leads us to thinking about what we should be doing with this precious gift. Shopping up a storm – for sure, making lots of money – definitely, but what then? But that is the subject of another book, perhaps even (though not necessarily) by another author.

Less is not more (more or less)

The subject here is a Wealth Journey. And first we must define wealth, which is quite a personal matter, different for each of the millions of people reading this book. (This is called creating a reality ... Yes, let me be clear – I want millions of copies of my books to sell around the world!) While wealth is definitely a broader concept than money, and puts us in mind of a state of being and a feeling and a way of life, we do not want to become so general or vague in our definition that we lose the plot. Wealth is wealth. It's not one of those 'less is more' things – unless you are simplifying. It's one of those 'more is more' things.

So, for a start, give a little thought to WEALTH.

- How would you know if you were wealthy?
- What would you have?
- How would you live?
- How would you feel?
- What would you be worth?
- Who would you be?

These answers will change over time. You may not be very clear about them right now, but that's okay. Because that's the whole purpose of a journey. You make a journey to discover new things, visit new places, find out aspects of yourself you did not know.

Let the journey begin! And it begins by finding out where you are.

1

Where You Are

The 9 levels of Wealth Consciousness

1. Ignorance
2. Blame
3. Struggle
4. Dependence
5. Co-dependence
6. Independence
7. Comfort
8. Wealth
9. Affluence

Before you begin a journey you must find out where you are. That is an obvious but profound truth. You absolutely cannot get anywhere unless you know where you are. No exceptions. Well, not unless you are on the train to nowhere – there are also cruises to nowhere.

Knowing where you are means assessing your condition, taking stock of things, in this case wealth. And because 'where you are' is closely linked to 'who you are' we need to start with that.

The 9 Levels of Wealth Consciousness present a version of reality according to me at this time, based on my experience in the wealth creation and transformation arena. It is a model, and like all models it does not have actual reality. Models are a way of our trying to make sense of the world. A good model can help you to see something – in this case wealth – in a totally different way.

The objective of the levels of wealth consciousness is not to compartmentalise yourself into yet another square box (*'Okay, so now I am Leo, no 1 Enneagram, extrovert, number 7 in numerology, with a choleric temperament, and I am in "Comfort" on the Wealth Consciousness scale.'*). The objective of my wealth model is to present a map to help you assess where you are, with a view to arriving at a new destination.

This model is a tool, nothing more. It is one of many possible versions of reality. How it works for you, is directly related to how much in agreement you are with it, and to what extent you embrace it. Decide now that you can use this tool to access deeper levels of yourself. Decide now that you will use this tool to expand your Wealth Consciousness and ultimately your wealth profile. It's a good decision!

Let's start with the first level, and work our way up.

1. Ignorance (is bliss?)(Daddy's little girl)

It's wonderful to watch little children before money has any value for them. At this stage they want 'a big silver money'. They do not understand the value of money, what it can buy or even why it is there. Later, when they understand that it can be exchanged for something, all they want to know is 'how many ice lollies is this?' Money still has no value for them.

Many adults remain in this state of 'wealth ignorance'. They pretend they do not understand money, or they don't want to understand it. They may say they are 'bad with money' because they are not 'mathematically minded' and other such nonsense. And so these individuals hide from money – never looking at it, always avoiding it, covertly needing and wanting it, but never confronting it.

Some people may in fact be genuinely ignorant about many aspects of money and how it works, but that is not the same thing. You need never know a thing about money beyond basic addition and subtraction, and you can become exceedingly wealthy. Many have. So it is not actual ignorance I speak of here. It is rather the ignorance of being in the dark, of putting your head in the sand like an ostrich, of not wanting to, nor daring to, nor bearing to look. It is the ignorance of not confronting something.

Are you one of these people? Well, money is coming to get you! No matter where you run, or where you hide! And, you know what, it's quite a loose-flowing, creative thing, money, if you know how to deal with it. Do not despair. All you need is the realisation that this is your Wealth Consciousness at this time, and the desire to change.

Sometimes ignorance is the result of culture, or upbringing. We are told not to talk about money, or that only one or other of the sexes can take care of the money. In the west it has been the man who takes care of the money, leaving the woman in ignorance. In Japan, it is the woman who takes care of the money – harking back to the days of samurai when it was considered undignified for the man to have anything to do with cash.

Way back in my early twenties I was living a wealthy and extravagant life. I was in a business which I had started with my then husband. We worked side by side and I ran the offices and staff. However, he was the one who handled all the money, signing of cheques and so on. I did not find this strange in any way. When I wanted money, I simply asked for it, and he gave it to me. I had always seen my mother and father interact in this way, so it seemed normal to me.

Many wives of wealthy husbands, and husbands of wealthy wives, also suffer from this syndrome of ignorance. My story did not have a very happy ending, though it did teach me to take my head out of the sand – which I clearly took to heart, as the writing of this book attests to!

In the space of a single afternoon I found myself literally penniless. My husband was assaulted, hospitalised, and in a coma. Meanwhile, I had a business to run. There were staff to pay, clients to service – and I couldn't even sign a cheque, or access our bank account. He never quite recovered, and was in and out of hospitals and mental institutes for a very long time.

Back at the office, I soon discovered huge debt – consignment stock sold but unpaid, company and his personal tax in arrears with massive penalties and so on. Suppliers withdrew credit facilities. I had to buy for cash and sell on terms. It took nearly two years to pay off everyone, and to put finances into the black.

I learnt a very big lesson. Many lessons in fact, but the key one, which relates to Wealth Consciousness, is DO NOT REMAIN IN IGNORANCE ABOUT MONEY MATTERS, or about anything, for that matter. And the more it matters, the more you should be looking at it.

When we ignore something it grows in shadow. While we avoid looking at something we cannot change it. When we look, we can see.

> What we can see, we can change,
> what we cannot see, we can do nothing about

Give a little thought to IGNORANCE.
- What am I ignorant about?
- What am I not facing with regard to money?
- What do I refuse to look at?
- What do I need to know about wealth that I don't?
- How can I face money?

What enlightened feeling do I want to feel?

*Take any decisions you need to take as a result of this knowledge. Formulate a plan of action and do it. Make any changes you need to make in your life. Keep it simple. **Connect to the feel-good feeling!** Keep it fun. This is a Wealth Journey.*

All you need is the realisation that this is your Wealth Consciousness at this time, and the desire to change. That is basically all. You don't need to dredge up every money-related incident in your childhood to justify your position or to put blame on someone else for the way you feel. Just see things for how they are. Decide you want to change.

Ignorance is avoidance. It is time to confront. It is time to act.

2. Blame (He did it!)

The next level on the Wealth Consciousness scale is Blame. At this point one has looked at money, but refuses to take responsibility for not having it, or in some cases, for having it. The levels of Wealth Consciousness are interwoven and holographic. In a sense, at each level you need to go through all the levels before you can get to the next one. For example, you can, while in Comfort, be stuck in Blame which keeps you from going to the next level of Power.

We love to blame. It's so easy. It makes so much sense. It's so convenient. Everyone can relate to it. There are so many people to blame too. Not just the people we know, obvious ones like partners, parents, siblings and relatives. There are teachers, staff, store attendants, even complete strangers. There are planetary conjunctions, ley lines, biorhythms and ancestors. There are world markets, the government, presidents of other countries and the oil price. There are laws, acts of God, economies, natural disasters, power failures and viruses. And if that's not enough, there are also past lives, extraterrestrials and conspiracies.

It's a real smorgasbord out there – you can take your pick! Or you can take responsibility. You will never make money while you sit around blaming anything or anyone – no matter how valid your reasons. Even if the buggers did mess it up, the question is not why they did it, or how they could have done it, or why they should fix it (because it's their fault, dammit!). The only question is, what are you going to do about it? What are You going to Do about it? Yes, *You!*

You cannot change anyone, or anything out there. It is

just not possible. You can only change yourself, and then everything and everyone out there changes too, because everything is connected. While you are in Blame you cannot take responsibility, and you cannot create change.

So many people who want to change the world spend an enormous amount of time and energy laying blame rather than making change. Blame is a resonance. It is very distinct, very de-energising. When you are in this state you are continuously disempowering yourself. You are continuously going out of your centre, out of your power. You are giving your power away to whatever is out there that you blame for your condition.

When you are in Blame you become smaller and more closed, you become the victim, and someone or something out there is causing things to happen in your life instead of you causing them to happen. People in Blame usually ask 'why?' a lot instead of 'how?' or 'what?'

Before attending any of my wealth creation courses, participants are required to complete a wealth questionnaire. The purpose is to help both participant and myself to prepare. One of the questions I ask is, 'If the money guru genie appears and grants you the answer to one question about money, what will that question be?' Many people want to know why they are not wealthy or why some people are wealthier than others or how we can use a different currency system to the one we have.

It is very much the minority who ask 'How can I get rich?' or 'What do I need to do to make money?' If you do not ask the right questions about money (or about anything for that matter), you will not get useful answers.

Blame is closely linked to laziness – for while you blame 'them' out there, you can also sit around and wait for 'them' to fix things. It's not your problem. You do not have to do anything. You don't need to take responsibility. The more irritated you become at reading this, by the way, the more you are really bursting at the seams to tell me how this is not true, and how there are certain circumstances where it *is* someone else's fault, then the more there is something you need to look at in this area.

Give a little thought to BLAME.

- Who do I blame for where I am in my life at present?
- Who do I blame with regard to money?
- What am I not taking responsibility for in the area of money?
- What am I hiding behind?
- How can I take responsibility for change, today?

What feeling would I feel if everything was okay?

Take any decisions you need to take as a result of this knowledge. Formulate a plan of action and do it. Make any changes you need to make in your life. **Feel the feel-good feeling!** *Keep it simple. Keep it fun. This is a Wealth Journey.*

The bridge between Blame and Responsibility is Forgiveness. It is a truly cleansing and liberating experience to let go of blame and grudge. It is often enough to simply think about anyone you need to forgive – their names or faces will pop up in your mind. Then, with the clear focus of your intent, decide to forgive them, right here and now in this moment. Say to them, in your mind, 'I forgive you'. Then let it go. Whatever 'it' is.

Imagine whatever disharmony stands between you as a ball of grey. Then see yourself throwing this grey ball into a glowing fire. Watch as the grey dissolves and transforms into golden light which is absorbed through your heart and the heart of the other person. Your bodies are filled with this light, which is energy and power. This is a very powerful and energetic transformation.

Decide right now, that your business with that person is finished. Release them, and release yourself. Decide it is over. Then move on. Let go of Blame. Decide to take Responsibility. Well done!

You are responsible. What are you going to do with the responsibility for your wealth? Remember, if you take responsibility, then you can decide that you can do anything you want to do. Because who can stop you if the responsibility rests with you? No one!

Give a little thought to RESPONSIBILITY.
- Who is responsible for creating wealth for me? *(If your answer is not 'ME', then go back to the Blame section.)*
- What can I do to take responsibility for the money in my life?
- How can I become totally responsible for creating wealth?
- What do I need to do to increase my level of responsibility in the area of money?
- What responsibility do I embrace in my life, today?

What feeling does embracing responsibility create for me?

Take any decisions you need to take as a result of this knowledge. Formulate a plan of action and do it. Make any changes you need to make in your life. **Connect to the feel-good feeling!** *Keep it simple. Keep it fun. This is a Wealth Journey.*

3. Struggle (Don't you *dare* give me that money!)

Why do we soooooo love to 'struggle'? With such nobility and pride? Why do we look askance at anyone who 'has it easy' – instead of saying 'Kudos to you, mate!'? Why do we scorn people who have 'things falling into their laps'? Instead of saying 'Well, well done!'?

I think it is part of the 'working hard' tradition of thinking. For many people, money is synonymous with struggle. Struggle, as a state of Wealth Consciousness is a state of denial. While in Struggle we are pushing and pulling, but not embracing, we are fighting with life, and with ourselves.

We are not embracing life, its bounty, ourselves, or others. While we struggle we cannot take an objective view of things. We have lost our perspective. We have become enmeshed in pain and suffering and we have become one-sided. We cannot see the light. We cannot see the end of the rainbow. We are stuck in and identify with our condition. We can become addicted to struggle, using it as a measure of our effort or even of our worth.

Many creative people seem to believe that the more they struggle, the more they suffer, the more indicative it is of their creativity. Many spiritual people believe that this 'struggle' is a true and necessary aspect of our life of suffering on this planet, and of our process of transcendence. What do you believe?

Wealth is a process of becoming

Give a little thought to STRUGGLE.
- What do I struggle with?

- Where and how am I fighting with the world?
- Which aspect of money making do I struggle with?
- Which struggle do I need to let go of?
- What am I not embracing?

How would it feel to flow?

*Take any decisions you need to take as a result of this knowledge. Formulate a plan of action and do it. Make any changes you need to make in your life. **Connect to the feel-good feeling!** Keep it simple. Keep it fun. This is a Wealth Journey.*

End the struggle. Embrace life. It's a decision, not an outcome. If your Wealth Consciousness is one of struggle, and you want to change it, you can. Right now! First acknowledge that this is your condition. Then decide to change it. That is all.

If Struggle forms a big part of your life, I recommend martial arts – t'ai chi or kung fu will help you cultivate the ability to flow, to channel resistance and even to redirect opposition so that it flows with you – or rather that you flow with it.

The need to struggle is deeply embedded in our psyches. It probably arises with the fight out of the womb, the struggle for that first breath. It is a survival urge – the urge to fight being the more active option of the fight/flight response which is encoded in our reptilian brain (that part of the brain which deals with automated, usually survival-related responses). Fight can help us to survive and overcome challenging situations. The problem arises when we become stuck in that fight state, in that struggle state, and we start to live our lives in that way.

Many people live that way. That's how we get road rage. The

urge to fight, if correctly channelled can be one of the secrets of success. But Struggle, as a level of Wealth Consciousness, and as a way of perceiving wealth and its creation, does nothing more than keep wealth away.

Imagine courting a potential lover. Imagine you want your lover to like and love you, to join you in your home, to live with you. You want to embrace them, welcome them, open your arms to them, invite them in. Now throw 'struggle' into that picture. It doesn't work, does it?

4. Dependence (Mommy's boys)

As children we are dependent on our parents for all our needs – food, clothing, housing, affection. They give and we receive. And as children we are unable to participate in any form of monetary exchange for what we receive – we do not work, or repay in kind, though we may be asked to perform chores in exchange for pocket money, later. When we are children, we do not know or worry about where our meals or clothes are coming from. We rest easily and comfortably in a warm cocoon of dependence, believing everything will be taken care of – which it generally is. It is a blissful form of ignorance based on trust.

Some adults never transcend this state. They rely, trust, and depend upon their parents or spouses (or 'the universe') to take care of them. Some live at home till they are old. Others drift around waiting for their inheritance to come into play. It is a condition of not growing up. It is a condition of not taking responsibility.

I have watched grown men in coffee bars allowing their aged mothers to pay the bill. This is Dependence. I have known (talented and capable) guys who can never hold down a job because they can't be that bothered – Mummy's always there to do the laundry and cook some meals – even when they are not living at home. That's Dependence.

I know children of the very wealthy who potter here and there, from time to time, with family money and little concern for the outcome. They know Daddy will bail them out, and he usually does. This is Dependence.

There is also the alternative practitioner, artist or musician, who refuses to advertise, or work a full day, or properly engage in the world, and claims the universe will take care of things. This is also Dependence.

There is a fine line between believing in, and allowing divine guidance to flow in one's life on the one hand, and taking responsibility for doing, on the other.

I'm sure you've heard the story of John the Devout. John believed in God and prayed faithfully every day, trusting that all his needs would be met. One day the floods came and it rained and rained and poured (and the wind howled). People began to evacuate the area. One by one, they offered to take John along in their cars, but John held firm, 'God will take care of me,' he said.

Slowly, all the neighbours were gone and John was all alone, but he continued to pray. 'Please help me, God.' The river began to rise, and wash the houses away, when a lone patrol car approached. 'Climb in, climb in, or you will drown,' said the policeman, but John would not budge. 'God will take care of me,' he said.

The water continued to rise around John to the second level of the house, when a boat came by. 'Climb in quickly, or you will drown,' entreated the man with the oars, but John refused and continued to pray.

Finally, when John's house was almost under water and

John was clutching on to the roof by the tips of his fingers, a helicopter flew by and released a long rope ladder that fluttered in front of John's head. 'Grab the ladder and climb,' shouted the pilot, 'or you will surely drown.' But still John declined. 'God will save me,' he said and he continued to pray.

Well, John drowned and went to heaven. There, quite distressed, he looked for God. 'Dear Lord,' he said, 'I believed in you devoutly my entire life, and I prayed and prayed, always trusting you would take care of me. But you let me drown. How could you let that happen?'

'My boy,' God replied, solemnly shrugging his shoulders, 'I sent you three cars, a boat *and* a helicopter!'

There is an old proverb,

'Trust in God, but tie your camel first'

Give a little thought to DEPENDENCE.
- Who or what do I depend on for my money?
- What is the one thing that I can truly depend on?
- Who depends on me?
- How can I broaden my field of wealth dependence?
- What do I need to do to become self-dependent with regard to wealth?

How would it feel to be independent?

Take any decisions you need to take as a result of this knowledge. Formulate a plan of action and do it. Make any changes you need to make in your life. **Connect to the feel-good feeling!** *Keep it simple. Keep it fun. This is a Wealth Journey.*

While you depend upon, or give responsibility to, someone else for your wealth, you will not be able to create it.

5. Co-dependence (Two halves do not make a whole)

Whereas most of the previous states were characterised by inaction, Co-dependence marks the beginning of doing.

Co-dependence is another form of Dependence, which is probably the condition of most middle-class people on the planet. In this form of dependence you are caught in a treadmill. Your earnings are used to pay off your many possessions. As your earnings increase, so does either the quality, or the quantity of your possessions.

The more money you earn the fancier and more expensive these possessions will become. The point is you are in Co-dependence. That means you need to keep the wheels rolling. You cannot stop, or retire. Your wealth, or current status, depends on your earnings. Money controls you here. At the same time you and your wealth are co-dependent on each other. Neither of you can exist alone.

Your wealth cannot flourish on its own. It has no existence apart from you keeping the wheels rolling. In Co-dependence, if you were to stop working, you would be unable to keep your house, your car and your lifestyle. Many people considered exceedingly wealthy are actually in Co-dependence. From time to time you hear of someone considered to be very wealthy actually being in huge debt, though they continue spending, and carry on living an extravagant lifestyle, until sometimes the wheels finally come off.

What does it mean when we say 'your wealth cannot flourish without you'? Well, it means that your wealth cannot stand alone. It cannot stand alone and you cannot stand alone, which is the definition of Co-dependence. It's like that much-used saying with regard to relationships about two halves making a whole. However, ideally, we are looking for a relationship where each whole becomes greater through the relationship than it would have on its own.

Having wealth that stands alone and is independent is like owning a house (fully paid up) and receiving rental from it. You maintain the wealth in the form of a house and ensure all is well. The house creates income for you. Both you and the wealth are better off with each other in the relationship. This can be contrasted with having a huge bond on a house that you cannot really afford and have to work twelve hours a day to repay. Moreover, if you were to stop the repayments, the bank would repossess the house. Wealth, as the house, has no existence without you in this case. And without it, you do not have the wealth either.

Co-dependence is not a very healthy relationship to have. It is like two people with crutches each supporting each other into some kind of whole. It's a parasitic relationship. In terms of a level of Wealth Consciousness the co-dependent relationship is also one where you use others and their money or connections or influence for the creation of wealth. Part of business you may say, and this is true to a point, but we are looking here at the resonance of a chronic taker and user, who mostly functions on this level.

In Co-dependence you believe the world owes you and is either there to be taken advantage of, or to pay homage to you. This is a more proactive form of not taking responsibility. It also extends, like all the levels of Wealth Consciousness, beyond the realm of wealth.

Co-dependence can become a form of addiction. We may

become addicted to anything from praise to needing to know we are the best. Whatever it is, in Co-dependence we are not free, and we are certainly not wealthy.

Give a little thought to CO-DEPENDENCE.
- In what way does my wealth reflect co-dependence?
- Who am I in a co-dependent relationship with?
- What am I receiving from my co-dependent relationships?
- How can I let go of or transform this need?
- What do I need to do to release myself from co-dependence?

How would I feel if I was free?

Take any decisions you need to take as a result of this knowledge. Formulate a plan of action and do it. Make any changes you need to make in your life. **Connect to the feel-good feeling!** *Keep it simple. Keep it fun. This is a Wealth Journey.*

People in Co-dependence usually do not see the state for what it is. They believe that this is the way things should be. In essence, this is nothing more than a prosperous manifestation of the struggle state.

6. Independence (Me, me, and little me)

Independence is the first truly active state of Wealth Consciousness. Here you have seen things for what they are and you want to change them.

Independence is first and foremost a decision. It is a turning point in life. It is a single moment in which you decide to turn things around, to take responsibility, to take charge of your life and of your wealth. It is the beginning of letting go. It could be this very moment, as you read these words.

Independence is the beginning of the Wealth Journey. Until this point, it has been preparation, letting go of excess baggage, shedding unnecessary weight so you can really move along.

Independence is also the realisation, the firm acknowledgement, that *you* are all you need and that you are enough! I remember the day many years ago when I suddenly knew that *I was the money*. I knew it did not matter where I went or what I did because where I was, there the money was with me, because I made the money and therefore *I was the money!* Even now, over twenty-five years later, saying those words still thrills and energises me! *I am the money! Yeah!*

> Independence is the realisation that
> you are all you need and that you are enough!

Independence is entered into when you decide you will make it happen. You will begin the Wealth Journey. This can take place at any point along the Wealth Consciousness track. You may then find yourself moving rather rapidly through the next few Wealth Consciousness levels.

In Independence you are taking responsibility. You are creating a future where you can be free from the money treadmill of debt-work-debt. Now is the time to look at budgets and investment options. Now is the time to become informed. Those of you who have read my *Money Alchemy* ™ and *Money Well* ™ books will remember me waving away budgets and strategies and financial planning. Well, now is the time for them.

You will find you will naturally be drawn to finding out

more about money. You will want to make informed choices, and I urge you to find out as much as you can about money and how it works before committing yourself in any way to any course of investment action. Call investment people in (yes, they must come and see you, not the other way around) to explain to you what they offer and how it works. Go to your bank and explore your options, get your bank to assign you your own personal banker. Ask, ask, ask. If you do not understand, ask again.

If the investment people you approach cannot explain, do not deal with them. Do not buy something if you do not know what it is or how it basically works. And if anyone tells you it's too complicated to explain, definitely do not deal with them. The basics of investment, whether it be in cash, equities (and its derivatives) or property are really simple enough for a child to understand, if explained clearly and properly. Most importantly, if any person who earns their living out of taking a percentage of yours makes you feel small, or intimidated, or stupid, or 'too scared to ask', dump them fast! This is good advice. Ignore it at your own peril.

Stand in your power

To maintain your status of Independence, you must be able to assert yourself. Stand in your power. That's what Independence is about. You must be able to think and act for yourself, and also to take responsibility for your actions. You must be able to trust yourself; most importantly, trust your gut. Trust your instincts above all things else. Trust that very tiny little whisper in your mind above all the fancy paperwork and familiar brand names and people who know better, even if they are better educated, wealthier, and more accomplished than you. This is also probably the best advice I can give you in this whole book.

The road to wealth which starts with Independence is paved with the pearls of your own wisdom. Begin to believe you know better. Because, when it comes to you, no one knows better than you what is best for you, and how best to get it. Begin to exercise that belief in your day-to-day life. Acknowledge and act on your intuition and it will get stronger and stronger. Say to your prospective investment person (even if it's just for a laugh), 'Thank you for coming but I don't think your product fits my investment requirements. I will call you. No, no, please don't call me, I'll call you.' Then giggle hilariously at your daring! Do it! Never forget to have fun!

As far as actual wealth is concerned, the consciousness of Independence is a little like a cocoon phase. It is the still point between one state and another. In Independence you are becoming aware, seeing things for what they are, taking stock, weighing your options and looking at possibilities.

Give a little thought to INDEPENDENCE.
- What do I need to experience to feel independent?
- What do I need to own and earn to be financially independent?
- In which area of my life do I enjoy independence?
- How can I increase my sense of independence in all areas of life?
- What do I need to do to become financially independent?

How would it feel to be free? (yes, again, for the third time!)

Take any decisions you need to take as a result of this knowledge. Formulate a plan of action and do it. Make any changes you need to make in your life. **Connect to the feel-good feeling!** *Keep it simple. Keep it fun. This is a Wealth Journey.*

Independence is the realisation that you
don't actually need money, because you are its source

7. Comfort (Well, this is nice . . .)

Comfort is the first real stage in the creation of wealth and in developing Wealth Consciousness. I believe it is the inability to contain this state that causes many people either not to acquire wealth or to crash back into levels below wealth once wealth has been acquired. Comfort is synonymous with contentment. It requires the ability to both be and to have.

In Comfort, you are free from worry about survival. Your debt is minimal or very much under control. You know what you want and have a plan on how to get it. You are breathing deeply and well. You may even have a smile on your face. Certainly you are comfortable. This is where you may have started to diversify your interests. You may have acquired a holiday home, or invested in the stock market. One of your cars is paid off and you own all your furniture. You have money in the bank.

In Comfort you have transcended Struggle and Blame and Co-dependence. You are taking responsibility for your life and its creation.

Many people choose to stay in Comfort as a life or path

choice. You will find some monks and nuns and people in service in this state. Being in service does not automatically put you here, though. Many people in service can also be in Struggle or Blame.

There is a subtle but huge distinction to be made between those who, having acquired a level of financial independence which is way beyond struggle and lack, choose to keep their lives simple, and those who have never transcended Struggle or Blame having no choice but to do the same. The difference lies in that little word, *choice*. (That's unless you have made a choice early on to simply serve – like Mother Teresa, for example – thereby transcending the whole wealth-creation cycle altogether.)

Whether it is true choice or not can only be clearly seen through the eyes of humility and honesty. If you have never been able to make ends meet, yet you secretly desire, in your deepest heart of hearts, something different from the 'simplicity' of your current life, then it is time to face the truth and change it. Do not fool yourself into believing that circumstances or consequences are a choice. Let the choice be one you make consciously, from a point of truth and strength.

There is always much debate on one of my courses when I mention that one cannot choose a simple life from a point of lack. Before you can know what enough is, you need to know what more than enough is. A hungry street child, deprived of food his whole life cannot tell you what constitutes a meal which is enough.

Now I am not saying you need to become exceedingly wealthy before choosing a simple life, but you certainly need to have experienced a life of plenty. You need to have grown through and transformed the various levels of Wealth Consciousness, which are also levels of personal development.

You need to know what it means and what it feels like to be comfortable (extremely comfortable), at the very least.

Some people scale down from Affluence or Wealth to Comfort as they grow older and want to simplify their lives. I have watched many of my old clients from my investment days do this. Some do it gracefully and with joy. Others see it as a shrinking and never quite enjoy it.

It is important to know what you want and need to feel prosperous and to be living the life of your dreams. It is important to peel out a lifetime of conditioning; all the input given by parents, friends, significant others, and the media in all its forms; and all the notions and mock-ups of what a wealthy, happy you looks like. You need to strip it all down, disassemble it, re-examine it, scrutinise it, and run it through your heart rather than your mind.

Then, if it is a super affluent lifestyle that you are after, complete with many mansions and at least four cars, or a really grandiose dream to help the earth, or to make a huge difference to the people on it, then absolutely go for it! Do not languish your days away in mere 'Comfort'; that would be a cop-out for you. And the thing about Comfort is that it is difficult to move out of, which is why the percentage of people who make it out of Comfort and into Wealth is truly fractional.

Trust your instincts above all things else

The percentage of people who stay in Comfort is also very small. Those who truly aspire towards and create a simple life; those who really know that they want very little; those who create masses of wealth for other causes but who have few needs themselves; and those most rare of people, the ones referred to in the Chinese writings as 'the ordinary man' – those who live simple, contented lives, are a truly tiny percentage of the population.

The ability to have, which is the ability to contain, which arises from the ability to simply be, is at the crux of contentment or the state of Comfort. Comfort is also about being comfortable in your body, in your life, in your possessions. It's about being comfortable to be you, and knowing what that you needs to be comfortable. My book *The Money Well™ – How to contain wealth* is very useful in this regard.

Find out as quickly as you can what it is you need. And if you are not an affluence seeker, do not waste years of your life acquiring things that you will only give away later. Strange advice to be giving in a book on money making, but there it is.

Give a little thought to COMFORT.
- Under what conditions do I experience comfort and contentment?
- What do I need to feel financially comfortable?
- Where do I experience discomfort in my life?
- How can I simplify my life?
- What do I need to do to become financially comfortable?

How does it feel to be comfortable?

Take any decisions you need to take as a result of this knowledge. Formulate a plan of action and do it. Make any changes you need to make in your life. **Connect to the feel-good feeling!** *Keep it simple. Keep it fun. This is a Wealth Journey.*

I remember a line out of 'Boston Legal' where Danny Krane (played by William Shatner) says to Alan Shore (played by

James Spader), 'It's really fun being me. Is it fun being you?'
Now *that* is the million dollar question!

Is it fun being you?

8. Wealth (Wealth! Wealth!)

So here you are, you have arrived, you are wealthy! Well done! This reminds me of something I once read about acquiring wealth. That there is a gradual progression from being poor and not knowing it, to being poor and knowing it, to being rich and not knowing it, to being rich and knowing it. In Wealth you are rich and are somewhere between not knowing and knowing it. And it is all relative to your ability to have, and to your view of reality, this term wealth.

The consciousness of Wealth
is the consciousness of no lack

As we said before, within each level of consciousness you will be going through the entire scale. Until your Wealth Consciousness is fully integrated you will hover between feeling and not feeling wealthy, no matter how much money you may have. There are many people who, while possessing enormous wealth, continue to retain a resonance of poverty. The Scrooge Christmas story is a good example of this. In my experience, it is not so much a matter of being mean or stingy, as it is an inability to accept and integrate the resonance of wealth. The Scrooges of the world actually believe that they are still poor. It's like anorexia (in reverse) in the money department.

Maintaining and containing wealth is stressful. Not just

in the obvious sense of more work, but also energetically. Money is a powerful energy force, it requires skill and focus to manage it. Attention is also required, as with anything else that is important. Your lover requires attention, so do your children, your horse, your pet, your garden, your talent in golf or music. Withdraw the attention and problems will arise – that is a given. Yet we somehow think that this should be different when it comes to money. Well, it is not.

More money requires more time, attention, responsibility, decision-making, choice, focus, containment, discipline, and care than less money does. Integrating the consciousness of wealth requires significant personal change too. Because wealth is not something you acquire, like a new car, or a fancy piece of jewellery. Wealth is a state of beingness, and expanding into that state is what the Wealth Journey is really all about.

Wealth is a process of becoming. The consciousness of wealth is the consciousness of no lack. It is embracing the fact that the world is an abundant place, and that there will never be a lack of anything in your life. That's a very scary thought, and produces anxiety in most people. The space of no lack, the space of abundance, is a space of pretty high resonance. And you need to let go of, or transcend, quite a lot to get there, as we have seen. Not only that, but you must face and overcome the 9 Wealth Challenges if you are to retain your wealth, moving up through the various levels from Ignorance all the way to Affluence.

According to Felix Denis, one of Britain's wealthiest self-made entrepreneurs, and author of *How to Get Rich*, Rich starts at a total asset value of 15-40 million pounds, what he calls The Lesser Rich. So clearly the concept of wealth is a very subjective one.

At Wealth your consciousness may expand to encompass global responsibilities. You may become concerned with the alleviation of world poverty and the nurturing of the planet. And certainly this is a symbiotic relationship because the more wealth you acquire the more the needs of others will beckon to you and the more able you will be to address them.

Once we have arrived at Wealth, we may need to ask ourselves different questions than before.

Give a little thought to WEALTH.
- Which global issues require my involvement?
- What change can I create in the world using my resources?
- Where should the focus of my attention be?
- How can I maintain and grow my wealth while benefiting the larger whole?
- What have I learnt that I can teach to enrich others?

How does it feel to be wealthy?

Take any decisions you need to take as a result of this knowledge. Formulate a plan of action and do it. Make any changes you need to make in your life. **Connect to the feel-good feeling!** *Keep it simple. Keep it fun. This is a Wealth Journey.*

When we arrive at Wealth, it is time to look at life from a broader perspective. It is time to look at our life purpose, and how best we can fulfil it. Because when we fulfil our life purpose, we move into Affluence.

9. Affluence (Into wealth and beyond . . .)

In Affluence you definitely know you are wealthy. This is an interesting thought, because it means that Affluence need not necessarily relate to having billions. Affluence is primarily a state of mind. It is a point of inner equilibrium, confidence, and freedom. It is a space of knowing you are the master of your fate. There is inner joy, gratitude and even elation at your good fortune. You have a sense of constant celebration – you are rejoicing at your good fortune and looking for ways to share this with others.

You are above all else in the resonance of appreciation and gratitude. It is no wonder that so many of the inspirational speakers and teachers put much focus on this point. Many books have been written on the subject of gratitude, because gratitude is a powerful force. And the more you resonate with gratitude, the more thankful you are for your good fortune, and the more you are drawn to share it with others, the more your affluence multiplies.

> When we fulfil our life purpose,
> we move into Affluence

I remember a time way back in my life when I owned very little. I lived in a studio apartment and worked mornings only, earning commission. I earned a lot of money, and my expenses were minimal (after overcoming initial setbacks). I felt free and totally abundant. I could come and go as I pleased, and there was no ceiling to my earnings. I had few responsibilities. I felt on top of the world.

My friend Barry was similarly blessed. We regularly met for lunch and ate enormous baked potatoes with our choice of filling in a tiny restaurant in Hillbrow in Johannesburg. We went off to Buddhist meditation retreats for many weeks at a time. We served the homeless at soup kitchens. And we celebrated our good fortune at every turn. We marvelled at how lucky we were to earn as we did and yet to have the freedom to come and go as we pleased. We were overjoyed and grateful. 'Isn't it amazing?' we would say every time we met.

I can honestly say that that was a time in my life when I felt more affluent than when my actual assets and bank balance reflected the fact. (I think I need to read this book ...!) And in fact, it was feeling this way that made it possible for me to attract the things that I did into my life, and create actual physical wealth to match my affluent mindset.

In Affluence you have the possibility to transcend. Not only because you have more money and independence, but because you carry the resonance of being able to create your environment – you can cause things to happen. In Affluence, your life works. You have the infrastructure and support to pursue any spiritual path you choose; to benefit any number of good causes; or to create your own new pathways that will alter the face of the planet.

In Affluence, you have power. How will you use it?

Give a little thought to AFFLUENCE.
- How can I best fulfil my life purpose and potential?
- What legacy do I want to leave behind when I am gone?
- Where should I show my gratitude?
- How can I best use all of my power for the benefit of all?
- What changes can I be making right now?
- What do I want to do with my life?

How does it feel to be healthy, wealthy and wise?

Take any decisions you need to take as a result of this knowledge. Formulate a plan of action and do it. Make any changes you need to make in your life. **Connect to the feel-good feeling!** *Keep it simple. Keep it fun. This is a Wealth Journey.*

The golden wrap

The 9 Levels of Wealth Consciousness provide a broad scale of wealth development which can be used to assess where you are on your Wealth Journey. Using your attention; intent to change; pure, open observation; and the questions provided; you can candidly assess your current position without judgement, and undertake to make empowering changes which will take you to the next level.

Keep it simple. *Connect to the feel-good feeling!* Have fun. And remember nothing is absolute.

Once you know where you are, your Wealth Journey has begun! Next, you must decide where you are going.

Wealth is a state of beingness, and expanding into that state is what the Wealth Journey is really all about

2

Where You Are Going

The 9 Dimensions of Self-Expression

1.	Physicality	*Cultivating Security*
2.	Identity	*Expansion of Self*
3.	Sexuality	*Reflection of Other*
4.	Creativity	*Expression of Flow*
5.	Spirituality	*Connection with Source*
6.	Authenticity	*Stepping into Uniqueness*
7.	Contentment	*Knowing what is*
8.	Service	*Following the call*
9.	Power	*Being the still centre*

The 9 Dimensions of Self-Expression are destinations of new beingness that we aspire to develop into.

This is the real destination of our Wealth Journey. We are ultimately trying to integrate and ground these nine expressions of being into one awesome self. And before we begin, it is good to reflect on the fact that we already contain these various expressions of self. They emerge and take focus in our lives at various stages of both our physical as well as our emotional and spiritual development.

As we put our consciousness and attention on the attainment of these expressions as an act of expansion of wealth and self, so we can better navigate our Wealth Journey. We also come to realise the deep-rooted emotional needs that our wealth quest is really trying to fulfil and in so doing become better equipped to fill those needs.

It is also important to remember that these aspects of ourselves coexist. So we are separating them for ease of reference only and also to highlight the fact that at various times in our lives and at various points along our Wealth Journey one or other aspect is highlighted or focused upon almost to the exclusion of the rest. That does not mean that the other aspects disappear.

The different aspects of self-expression must be looked upon as different layers of a spiral-shaped three-dimensional onion. And if you can imagine that, you will certainly be able to pass through the eye of a needle – hump and all! It's important not to take any of this too seriously. It's important to take the time to giggle (and sneeze)! Bless you!

Physicality is where and how we root ourselves
It is how we become grounded in the world

1. Physicality – Cultivating Security

We begin the Wealth Journey wanting money and all manner of physical, tangible things. We want assets and cars and trips overseas, and a helicopter and maybe a yacht. Even before that we may want a roof over our heads (that we own) and clothes and food on the table. And most of this tangible wealth is associated with the feeling of being secure in the world. Very much in the same way as we develop our bodies from infanthood to adolescence and then to adulthood. The physical expression of wealth – the clothing and housing and feeding of ourselves – is where all Wealth Journeys start.

This is one of the foundations of our journey. It is where and how we root ourselves. It is how we become grounded in the world, and so it is important that attention is paid here. It is important that the right habits and beliefs and patterns are put into place, for without firm foundations, the top (once it is created) will no doubt topple.

What does this mean in reality? What it means is that owning a yacht when the food on your table is paid for on credit is not appropriate. Now, much of the planet lives this way. They actually cannot afford the food on their table. They are paying for it by debt – credit card and overdraft and financial gearing or leverage (financing capital through outside lenders or shareholders).

And note how confusing our language is around this topic. Note how a credit card is actually a debit card, or more accurately a debt card. A debit card (with which you actually make immediate payment) should be called the credit card. Consider how many people would be proud to flash around their platinum debt card, if that was what it was called.

But let's get back to physical wealth, this being the

expression of self we are going for on this level of our Wealth Journey. In order to create and cultivate good sound roots, we need to make sure we create credit and assets – in every way, while on this level.

We need to clarify our thinking around how we operate our life and our wealth. We need to create a life filled with assets, with what we can contain and with what we can afford. We need clear parameters. We need to decide what we really want. And we need to be *clear* about what we really want – both the physical stuff and the emotions that go with that physicality.

On the dimension of physicality we want to feel safe in the world. Often, at this level, there may be concerns about loss and theft. There may be much fear around both having and not having wealth. My first two books – *Money Alchemy*™ and *The Money Well*™ deal with these aspects at length and provide suitable processing to transcend these states and emotions.

Central to every dimension of self-expression is that we seek not only the wealth, but the key to unlocking the inner quality that that level represents. In physicality that quality is security.

Reflect on Security

- What do I need to feel secure in the world?
- What activities make me feel safe?
- What do I need to own to feel secure? List what you want.
- What does wealth mean to me in physical terms?
- What can I do to feel more secure, today?
- What will I have, when I am secure?

Connect with the feeling of Security

- Where is it in your body?
- What image or picture represents it?
- What activities invoke it?

Commit to absorbing and cultivating a sense of security **in your world.**

> All the security and safety you need
> is hidden deep within you

2. Identity – Expansion of Self

The cultivation and expansion of Self is what the whole Wealth Journey is all about. And the awareness of that self emerges for the first time as the second dimension of self-expression. Even as you begin to aspire towards and accumulate and even acquire physical possessions and the security these bring, you become aware that it is a new you that you are in fact aspiring to become.

Beyond and intertwined with the physicality of the Wealth Journey is the quest for a new self. This is a topic very central to my approach on wealth creation, and is woven throughout my writing. When we begin a Wealth Journey what we are really looking for is a new self. This new self simplistically speaking is a more wealthy self, but it is also someone who is different and who feels different from the self at the start of the Wealth Journey.

What we really want is how our wealth will make us feel

It is important to discover not only where you're going but also who you're trying to become. And, even more importantly, how you are hoping that that new you and the increased wealth will make you feel. Because what we are always after is a feeling. What we really want is how our wealth will make us feel.

The feeling we hope wealth will bring is different for everyone. Some people want to feel secure, others want more power. For some wealth means more freedom to do exactly as they please. Indeed, we often connect eccentricity with wealth. Some people want wealth so they can feel more attractive, less insecure, more creative.

Find out what more wealth means for you. Find out who you are trying to become and what you are trying to feel with your extra currency. This is the beginning of your journey of self-awareness which will be expanded upon over and over again as you progress along the various dimensions of self-expression.

The process of wealth creation begins with a realisation that it is the I who is the self without wealth wanting to change into the I who is the self with wealth. Somewhere along the Wealth Journey comes the clear knowledge that 'I am the creator of the wealth', 'The wealth comes from me'.

Your Wealth Journey through the various levels of self-expression is a continuous deepening and grounding of that fact. Begin by reflecting on that fact, and on the feelings and beingness you are hoping wealth will provide an opportunity for.

It is important to discover not only where you're going
but also who you're trying to become

Reflect on Feeling Wealthy

- What feeling do I want wealth to provide?
- Who do I want to become when I am wealthy?
- What does a wealthy me feel like?
- What has a wealthy me overcome?
- What is a wealthy me free to express?

Connect with the feeling of Wealth-Being™

- Where is it in your body?
- What image or picture represents it?
- What activities invoke it?

Commit to absorbing and cultivating a sense of Wealth-Being™ **in your daily life.**

Once you have discovered what the wealthy you feels like, practise feeling that way as much and as often as you can. The feeling will attract the wealth to you faster than any action plan will. Try it!

3. Sexuality – Reflection of Other

The next level or expression of wealth is sexuality. Many people equate the acquisition of wealth with a partner or partners, a love affair or affairs, or the easy conquest of desirable and attractive people. And, indeed, we see evidence of this all around. The wealthy toads do indeed marry beautiful princesses even without turning into princes first (and vice versa) ... It is one of the privileges that wealth brings.

So we may seek wealth as a means of enhancing our sexuality. We may be trying to become wealthier because we think that that will ensure a good partner, or make us more attractive to a good partner. (And it does …)

In seeking and exploring this path, we are in fact exploring that aspect of ourselves that reflects itself in others and is reflected by others. We are looking for mirrors. We are looking to integrate our inner male or female. We may also be exploring the parameters of our society in terms of archetypal roles of male/female in terms of earning and support.

In fact when we enter the level of Sexuality we begin to look at our support structure for wealth in the world. Many of the women I see in my practice are questioning and grappling with finding their place with respect to wealth and earnings in their marriages and partnerships.

Which relationships does wealth reflect?

Many issues arise when you reflect on wealth from the perspective of intimate relationships, partnerships and marriage. The traditional roles of male as primary earner and female as supportive housewife and mother are being challenged by both men and women.

Whereas some time back women fought for the right to earn alongside men, today many of these same women are questioning the validity of staying at home, especially when children arrive. In addition, the earning capacity of many women surpasses that of their men. This too leads to many questions around support, what it is to be a man or woman, roles in the marriage or partnership, and control.

Some men take on the role of house-husband, taking care of the home and children while the woman goes to work. In other cases, both parties take responsibility for the children in turn, working and caring together.

At the same time, there are men (and women) who believe that women should stick with their traditional role of keeping house, home and entertainment going for their man, while the man spoils and supports her. Some wealthy men believe that the woman should also work and do her part. They run their marriages like a business, dividing everything straight down the line in terms of money coming in and money going out.

When we explore Sexuality as the destination for our Wealth Journey we need to reflect on many of these aspects. I want to point out again that these aspects of self-expression coexist and are intertwined. So although for some the sexual aspect of their Wealth Journey is the sole focus for their destination, for most it is not only just one part of the computation, it is also a process of transcending and integrating levels of self.

Ultimately all journeys, including the Wealth Journey are about an exploration and deepening knowledge of who we are and what we want from life. Knowing this as it relates to significant others is quite an important part.

Reflect on Wealth & Relationships

- What link do I make between money and relationships?
- How would being wealthy make me more sexually attractive?
- What is my financial role in my relationship?
- How do I see my partner's financial role in the relationship?
- What is the role of man/woman in a relationship?
- What is the role of money in a relationship?
- How does money reflect my relationships?
- If money was my significant other, what would it say about me?

Connect with the feeling of being loved and accepted

- Where is it in your body?
- What image or picture represents it?
- What activities invoke it?

Commit to absorbing and cultivating a sense of being loved and accepted **in your daily life.**

4. Creativity – Expression of Flow

Once we feel safe in the world, start to explore our sense of self and connect with Other, we begin to expand our life further outward, and to extend our connectivity into the broader whole. We start to express and experience ourselves in terms of Creativity. Indeed one of the most common things people who are contemplating making a career change say to me is –'I want to explore my creativity. I want to do something more creative.'

Now it's a sad state of affairs that we should not consider our work as that thing which is creative and fulfilling. It is a sad reflection of the collective viewpoint on money and earnings that many feel earning a living is something separate from and not connected with their creative juices. This is the type of thinking my work is aiming to transform.

Many of us see wealth as opening doors to our creativity and enabling us to live life and to work differently. This is certainly the case. With money you can take time out to write and paint and compose and direct and train in surfing. There is no doubt whatsoever about that.

However, there is also a lot of evidence to support the fact that when you pursue that thing which you love to do with focus and intent and passion, you will be successful in that thing. All it takes to get on track is courage, belief in miracles and wonders and focused intent.

Take me as an example. I decided to first earn and become financially independent before I went off to write and teach. Of course my journey though the business world and the world of transformation has played a huge role in enabling me to gain first-hand experience around my subject and to create workable processes and a really unique, holistic approach to wealth creation. Also, the fact that I can, and have, created enormous wealth for myself and others, certainly adds huge credibility to the validity of my approach.

However ... yes, lately the however has occurred to me ... however, had I started writing way back then – if not straight after school, then after my first business experience in my late twenties – imagine where I'd be today. Imagine how much I could have written and created. That thought occurs to me, yes, it does.

Sure, my work may have developed differently, perhaps I'd be teaching energy differently, who knows? But one thing I know for sure – I could have done it. I could have just started writing and teaching. Just like that. From the beginning. From the word go. It may not have been as ideal as the path I actually took (from many perspectives), but it was definitely a doable course of action, which would also have produced superb results.

Most of the top creative people in our world devote their lives to creating in their chosen field. That's why they become the best. They don't first take time out to study for a degree 'to fall back on'. And let me just say how much of our language needs to change! Why do we need to fall, so requiring something to fall on? Why do we need to go back, or fall back? Why are we not encouraged to study that thing that we can move forward towards, or 'fly up to'?

So, for many people the creative world is what the destination of their Wealth Journey is all about. They want time to create, whether it's a work of art or a piece of music or whether it's a business or a family. Creating a family is, in fact, a highly creative act, something we often overlook.

What we need to recognise is that we create all the time, in many different ways and that we can create whatever we want, wherever we are. When our every step through life is a beautiful dance, then the flows of creation are indeed open, and will result in more flow towards and around us.

We also need to believe that wealth and creativity do in fact go together. We need to cultivate and put energy into that thought form. We must bring that new thinking into being. We need to create sayings like, 'Don't go for a business degree, there's lots more money to be made in music' or, 'Writing? That's fabulous! Lots of money to be made in that' or, 'Why don't you rather pursue your dancing?' We need to start assessing our life work in terms of how much thrill and joy it generates for us. We need to say to our children, 'Surfing is what you really enjoy, so why not do that for a living? You could teach, become a champion, or open a surfing store.' Then we need to give them the skills to survive and excel in that, their chosen field.

Going back (or forward) into Creativity as the destination of our Wealth Journey, we reflect on what creativity means for us, and what feeling that creativity inspires.

Reflect on Creativity

- How do I express my creativity in my daily life?
- Which areas of my creative self am I not containing?
- What aspect of creativity do I want wealth for?
- How can I incorporate creativity into my work?
- What am I trying to express?
- How much of my life am I creating?
- How does being creative feel?

Connect with the feeling of creation

- Where is it in your body?
- What image or picture represents it?
- What activities invoke it?

Commit to absorbing and cultivating a sense of being the creator **in your daily life.**

When we create, we become in charge of our world – that is what we try to capture with our creativity.

5. Spirituality – Connection with Source

In many spiritual paths it is considered extremely fortunate to be born wealthy, as this gives one the opportunity to pursue one's spiritual path. Wealth is considered to be the result of much past karmic good, and the purpose of wealth is seen as the deepening of one's spiritual practice. Indeed, a wealthy person who has no need to stress and toil for food or lodgings is free to pursue their enlightenment, and to help with the enlightenment of others.

And whereas we do see some of the rich and famous

engaged in wine, (wo)men and song, by far the majority have a keen awareness of the need to deepen their spiritual practice and to help those less fortunate than themselves.

Once we have acquired sufficient wealth to deal with our physical needs (in excess, naturally ...), our relationships, and broader aspects of creativity like business, children, or creativity itself, the need to express our spirituality emerges. For many, it is this need itself which inspires the Wealth Journey in the first place. For some, money is nothing more than the means through which they can follow God. And in a very general sense that is the case for all of us.

You don't need much money (at all) to connect with God!

At some point we question whether there is more to life than the visible, than our work and home and play, and it is at this point that Spirituality and our connection to source is explored. For many, it is at this point that new career choices are contemplated, or the change of life partners, or home.

There is a quest for meaning, and it is here that the seeds for service are sown. This questing is what was traditionally known as the mid-life crisis, and it usually comes any time between the early forties and the mid-fifties. In cultures of old, people were supported through this period of crisis, both materially and emotionally. It was understood that this is a rite of passage, and the beginning of coming into one's power.

In Vedic culture the head of the home (usually the man) would leave householder life (his wife and family) and head for the hills when he was somewhere in his fifties (once children had grown up and started their own families), in pursuit of his spiritual practice. This was understood to be a good and proper thing to do. (In Sanskrit the word *veda* means knowledge and the Vedic culture, based on the sacred texts of the Vedas, flourished all over the ancient world.)

Of course if spiritual practice of any kind is something that draws you, why not save time and lots of energy, and simply join a church, ashram or path where you can be supported while you practise, in exchange for service?

If you are trying to create wealth as a means of deepening your connection with God, start to practise today! You don't need much money (at all) to connect with God!

Reflect on Spirit

- How do I express my spirituality in my daily life?
- Which part of my spirit am I not containing?
- What aspect of spiritual practice do I want wealth for?
- How can I incorporate my spiritual practice into my work?
- Which aspect of spirituality do I want wealth for?
- How do I stay connected with Source?
- How does being spiritual feel?

Connect with the feeling of Connection with Source

- Where is it in your body?
- What image or picture represents it?
- What activities invoke it?

Commit to absorbing and cultivating a sense of the Spiritual **in your daily life.**

When we are connected with Source, with the Divine spark within, then the path towards our wealth becomes truly illuminated

6. Authenticity – Stepping into Uniqueness

The search for Authenticity is a lifelong one and it is apparent at every step along the Wealth Journey. In one sense we can say that that is where the Wealth Journey both begins and ends. But discovering our uniqueness and truly stepping into it and owning it is something not all of us achieve.

> Authenticity is about walking life in a way that always
> resonates with, and remains true to who you are

Yet Authenticity is no doubt a big inducement for our journey. Many of us want wealth so we can freely express who we are without reservation, and although this subject was touched upon earlier in the section on 'Identity – Awareness of Self', this is a much higher resonance of that expression. What began as basic differentiation is now being cultivated into a quality from which Power will emerge.

Authenticity is not only about recognition of self, or about integrating both sides – the light and the shadow – Authenticity is about walking life in a way that always resonates with and remains true to who you are. This means right speech, right action, right livelihood, right thinking. It means no compromising with ourselves and what is right for us.

This is a very freeing state of mind. It is very clear and very open. And we do not need wealth to attain it. The interesting thing about the various levels of self-expression that we try to acquire with wealth, is that we very soon come to see that the higher up we go the less wealth we *actually* need. This may seem a strange thing to read in a wealth creation book, but it's true none the less.

The less we compromise on who we are and what we need,

the clearer our resonance and flow, the easier for things to flow from, through, and to us. Energy and flow cannot work when they have been distorted and suppressed and reshaped into what they are not. We don't see nature ever behaving this way. We never see a rose trying to be a daffodil. We never see a fish trying to be an eagle, or an oak tree trying to become a rock (not unless it's petrified, that is – interesting, how that happens to us too ...)

Yet we spend our lives trying to be who and what we are not. We do everything from changing the colour and shape of our hair to re-contouring our bodies to trying to live in places that are not conducive to our health. We try to act in ways that will please our partners, hold off saying anything that will displease our boss, and put up with all manner of indignities and unacceptable-ness and shrinking and maligning of our person to the extent that we need therapy to tell us we are okay! And then we still don't believe it for the first seven years of treatment!

What are we thinking? Who are we trying to be? Who are we trying to become?

We think wealth will make everything okay. That with wealth we will suddenly be able to accept and love ourselves. We believe that with enough money we will no longer run the internal hate speech that disempowers and shrinks us. We think money will make everything okay.

Well, it will not.

You need to discover, connect with, and practise living in harmony with your Authenticity. That is the true well of wealth.

Reflect on Authenticity

- Who is my authentic self?
- Which part of my authenticity am I not containing?
- Which part of my authenticity am I hiding from the world?
- Where do I compromise my beingness?
- How am I not true to myself?
- What needs to happen for me to feel free to be me?
- How does being authentic feel?

Connect with the feeling of Authenticity

- Where is it in your body?
- What image or picture represents it?
- What activities cultivate it?

Commit to absorbing and cultivating a sense of Authenticity **in your daily life.**

The call to Authenticity is initiated by your connection with Source. When you enter into or deepen your spiritual practice, you connect with that part of you which is Divine, authentic and true. Now you must walk in that truth.

Authenticity is the true well of wealth

7. Contentment – Knowing what is

Contentment is containment. It is peace. It is knowing that all is as it should be. All is well. Everything is fine. Contentment is knowing what is. And when you really know what is, you are fully in the present and looking at the way things are without judgement.

On our path of transformation, whichever path that may be, we are really trying to do two things – come into the present and accept what is, as it is. The two are synonymous. Most of our pain and suffering comes from not accepting those two conditions. Either we are caught in the past in some or other way, or we will not accept the way things are in the present. And before we can try to change the situation, we need to see what is there.

When our attention and energy and power are caught in the past, we cannot function properly. We get caught in the past because our minds get stuck on some old incident, or we believe our thoughts about something, or we are reminded of some old thought or emotion or painful incident and plunge into reliving it, or we follow an old track, one that our mind is well grooved into running along, almost without thinking.

Being stuck in the past is not conducive to contentment. Contentment is synonymous with containment and we can only contain what is here. We cannot contain what is not – the past, or what we do not want. We can also only be content in the here and now. Contentment is the sense of being full and being okay. It involves a high degree of self-acceptance.

It's okay, you're okay, and everything is fine

That does not mean we do not change anything. What it means is that we can see what is there but we do not need to be sucked into it, fight it, run away from it. We observe what is, quite openly and with contentment, and then we make whatever changes we see fit to that.

Often we are so caught up in the past or in our stories

that we do not see what is there. We do not accept, we do not appreciate, we do not see. Often we are living a wonderful life but our mind is running a different story to reality and we cannot see reality for what it is.

Often we have enough, we are living a good life, supported by good people who love us, we have the luxury of holidays and gifts and friends, yet we are filled with discontent and unhappiness. We take small, irrelevant aspects of our life and magnify them into huge problems.

We become delusional, thinking a bit of excess weight, or a couple of wrinkles, or the fact that our husband watches too much television or does not buy us flowers or never cooks, or the fact that our wife cooks too much, thereby making us overweight, is some sort of huge insurmountable obstacle to our happiness and well-being.

THEN, we irrationally conclude that what we *really* need is more money! Then we would lose weight, fix the wrinkles, get a health chef and order our own flowers. This is what we think. And it's nothing more than a silly story.

We need to really look. Pay attention. See what's there. Embrace our lives. Become content with what we have, with who we are, with life, with the sunrise and sunset. We need to recognise that soon we will be dead. We are here but for a fleeting moment – and then it's gone. And no matter what your belief system: whether you believe you will reincarnate onto this planet or another, or go to heaven (or hell), or that it all just ends – Kaput! – you certainly won't know the final answers in the here and now (if you know what I mean). So, really, put down this book and celebrate what you have, and start to be happy with it.

It's okay, you're okay, and everything is fine. There is nothing you need to do to better yourself! When you really grasp that, you can throw out all your transformational books (including this one) and head for the beach. That's what the seagulls do. And they should know.

There is nothing you need to do to better yourself

Reflect on Contentment

- What am I not appreciating in my life?
- What am I not seeing for what it is?
- What gives me a sense of contentment?
- How do I create discontent in my life?
- How do I measure contentment?
- What needs to happen for me to feel content?
- How does being content feel?

Connect with the feeling of Contentment

- Where is it in your body?
- What image or picture represents it?
- What activities create it?

Commit to absorbing and cultivating a sense of Contentment **in your daily life.**

When we discover the key to our contentment, we will discover the key to wealth.

8. Service – Following the call

So very many people express a desire to serve the greater whole – the humanitarians of the world, social workers and environmental activists, health professionals and healers, energy workers and performers, politicians and animal lovers as well as the average man and woman in the street.

I am writing this book because I am one of those people. And I began writing wealth creation books because of the very many people I encountered in my own life who were keen to serve, yet were always strapped for cash.

We all seek to serve, one way or another. It is almost a primal need which arises out of our connection with one another and our connection with the greater whole. We are all connected because we are all energy and we are all part of the Divine spark.

Our desire to serve takes many forms. From the service of parents towards their children to the service performed by nurses, doctors, teachers, fire fighters, police, garbage-disposal people and all those who maintain the structure of our society. Some serve the world through great inventions that make the world a better place or save lives. Others serve through enlivening our spirit through wonderful works of art or literature or music. Still others create and run enormous corporations that serve through employing thousands of people thus feeding and clothing them and keeping them alive.

We all serve and we are all in service. No service is more important, or more noble than any other. Not really. We need to recognise and respect the fact that we all serve ourselves and one another as best we can. We need to extend the attitude and intent of service to everything we do.

And when we come to our Wealth Journey with the intent to serve the greater whole – no matter whether that is through providing tailor-made suits or building homes for the poor – we certainly open up and speed up the journey.

There is nothing else to do here on this planet, really, other than to serve the greater whole. And it should be our intent, our prayer and our mission to put all our skills, talents, abilities, gifts – in fact the full measure of our Authenticity – towards serving the greater whole.

Because when we serve the greater whole we serve ourselves and then the greater whole serves us too. More and more people are realising this simple fact, which is why we are experiencing so much expansion at this time.

Reflect on Service

- How can I serve the greater whole?
- Where am I drawn to serve?
- What gives me a sense of service?
- Who most needs my unique blend of talents and skills?
- Where would my life make a difference?
- How does being in service feel?

Connect with the feeling of Service

- Where is it in your body?
- What image or picture represents it?
- What activities cultivate it?

Commit to absorbing and cultivating a sense of Service **in your daily life.**

You can decide to serve in so many ways – the choice is yours. What is important is your intent to be a contributing part of the greater whole.

> When we serve the greater whole, we serve ourselves,
> and the greater whole serves us too

9. Power – Being the still centre

Everyone wants Power. And we see how it can corrupt and poison – especially those 'in power'. So what does it mean to have Power, and how do we get there in terms of our Wealth Journey, for there is no doubt it is the reason many people want to get to wealth.

Many people feel very powerless in the world and they think that more money would fix that. That is true to a point, and it's also one of those paradoxical catch-22s. For in order to make more money, you need to become more powerful in the world in many different ways. The way you become more powerful, the qualities you need to cultivate and integrate and the pathways you need to travel, are in fact the subject of this book.

Power is recognising the still centre within

This book, my work, is all about becoming empowered. It is a word very often used after my sessions or courses. People feel more empowered. What does that mean? It is nothing more than the awareness that their power is within, that they are the ones with the power.

Power is recognising the still centre within. That is all. The still centre within cannot be created or destroyed. It is not affected by what goes on around it. It is contained and it is present. The still centre within has been and is always with us. We simply need to remember it is there.

Power is the recognition that we are creating what goes on around us, and therefore we can change it. Power is finding our direction, activating our intent and mobilising our will.

Power is what this book will give you (or rather activate within you), if you read it and do the work.

Power is knowing you have power, no matter how much money is in the bank, because you are the creator of the money. Power is remembering who you are, and that it's okay. Power is knowing that you can have the life you want, that you have choice, and that you can exercise that choice.

Power is changing your story, expanding beyond it. Power is embracing change. Power is having fun, laughing, becoming like a little child again – because who wields more power in this world than a newborn infant?

Power is knowing that you know best what is right for you and for your journey. Power is the proper use and flow of energy. Power is allowing and bending and yielding effortlessly like a tree.

You have the Power

Reflect on Power

- How can I connect with my power?
- Where do I lose or leak power?
- What gives me a sense of power?
- What does having power mean to me?
- How can I best use my power to serve?
- How does having power feel?

Connect with the feeling of Power

- Where is it in your body?
- What image or picture represents it?
- What activities invoke it?

Commit to absorbing and cultivating a sense of Power **in your daily life.**

You have the Power. Use it.

In the next section you will learn how to identify and integrate the various wealth challenges you face along your path to wealth and how to overcome these through integrating the gifts they offer so that you can move effortlessly from the one level of Wealth Consciousness to the next.

Why You Are Not There

The 9 Wealth Challenges – and how to unlock their potential

1. **Avoidance : Confront**   Key: Courage
                                 Root: Perseverance
2. **Denial : Responsibility**   Key: Truth
                                 Root: Honour
3. **Struggle : Embrace**   Key: Flow
                                 Root: Allow
4. **Control : Expand**   Key: Generosity
                                 Root: Openness
5. **Complicate : Simplify**   Key: Choice
                                 Root: Knowledge
6. **Dissipate : Contain**   Key: Purpose
                                 Root: Service
7. **Daydream : Create**   Key: Action
                                 Root: Grounding
8. **Dictate : Direct**   Key: Vision
                                 Root: Clarity
9. **Power : Transcend**   Key: Appreciate
                                 Root: Divine Connection

In order to move successfully from one level of Wealth Consciousness to another, and ultimately to arrive at where you're going, you need to overcome various challenges. Although these challenges correlate with each level of Wealth Consciousness, they may present at any point along the Wealth Journey.

Each level of Wealth Consciousness contains a challenge of opposites which have to be integrated in order for an empowering quality to emerge. This empowering quality is the key to unlocking the challenge.

The holographic nature of this wealth model allows the whole range of challenges to present within one level of Wealth Consciousness. This means that you may, on the level of Wealth, have to once again deal with the challenge of Avoidance, but now you will be doing so on a much 'higher' level.

Developmental challenges occur throughout life. They provide tools that help us to grow. As babies we have to push our way out of the womb, down the birth canal and into a new world where we fight for our first breath. We go through the pain of teething, we struggle through childhood ailments to boost our immune system, we ache as our bones grow. These physical changes all represent and herald a change in emotions, thinking, and consciousness. Developmental challenges represent evolution and growth, and the struggle we undergo to enter into each new space provides us with tools and makes us stronger.

So it is with the Wealth Challenges. Bearing in mind that our Wealth Journey is a journey of acquiring inner as well as outer wealth, Wealth Challenges give us the tools that will help us to reach the next level on our Wealth Journey.

Let us look at the Wealth Challenges now and see how we

can transcend and integrate them, making our passage into wealth smoother and more skilful.

> Power is finding our direction, activating our intent
> and mobilising our will

1. Challenge: *Avoidance – Confront*
Key: *Courage*
Root: *Perseverance*

The first challenge on the Wealth Journey is Avoidance. This challenge closely correlates with Ignorance – the first step on the Wealth Consciousness scale. However, Avoidance is not confined to this level only, and may recur at any point along the Wealth Journey.

All types of Avoidance have one thing in common – the inability or unwillingness to confront. Confrontation requires courage. Courage is the ability to face *whatever is there*. The problem is we only want to look at nice things, positive things, happy things, things that make us feel good. So when faced with a problem we would rather ignore it. We do not like to hear or say no.

This can become a real problem.

Embarking on the Wealth Journey, like embarking on any journey, requires courage. It is not for pansies. If you cannot bear to hear the word NO without wilting, if you cannot bear to *say* the word NO without cringing, then stay at home. This is good advice, really. You will save yourself a lot of time and trouble.

> Courage is the will and determination to move forward,
> to act, despite fear

Ability to confront is the absolute cornerstone, the foundation, of wealth creation. I cannot stress this enough.

Good foundations are what will determine your ability to arrive at your wealth destination. If you cannot face or acknowledge the fact that you are actually struggling financially and not living a life of creative simplicity, then you will be unable to move beyond this point. If you cannot say 'No' to the persistent salesperson on the telephone when you do not need his product, then what will you do when you are faced with having to fire a dishonest employee who is putting your whole company at risk (even though he has a family to support)?

Richard Branson, in his book *Screw it, Let's do it*, tells the story of acquiring his island by offering the seller a ludicrously low sum of money (all Branson could afford at the time), and then repeating his offer, which was rejected several times before being accepted. You cannot do that without courage. You cannot do that without the ability to have 'No' roll off your back. You cannot do that without the ability to confront.

We will now process around the challenge of Avoidance with a view to cultivating the ability to confront, through our raised awareness. As always, complete these tasks with a slightly detached air. Do not judge yourself. Set your intent on the willingness to learn and integrate this challenge.

Let's take a look at *AVOIDANCE – CONFRONT*
(Write for 2 minutes on each)
- What do I avoid as a general pattern in my life?
- What am I really trying to avoid or not confront?
- How do I avoid wealth?
- How do I avoid confronting the things I do not want to face?

- Which words, phrases, mannerisms, gestures, facial expressions do I use when I refuse to confront something?
- Which emotions arise when I refuse to confront?
- Which emotions am I trying to stifle when I refuse to confront?
- Where do I lose my power in these confrontations?

Underline important words and phrases and summarise into one sentence.

How would it feel to be able to face anything?

Take any decisions you need to take as a result of this knowledge. Formulate a plan of action and do it. **Feel the powerful feel-good feelings!** *Make any changes you need to make in your life. Keep it simple. Keep it fun.*

Transcending AVOIDANCE – *The gift of* COURAGE *through* PERSEVERANCE

Courage is not the absence of fear. Courage is the will and determination to move forward, to act, despite fear. This is a very important point. In every tale involving a hero, we come to a point in the tale when the hero must perform a task that seems to be quite beyond him. At the root of all courage is perseverance.

After surviving many life-threatening challenges, at the end of his strength and tolerance, when it seems that there is no will left to continue, our hero is suddenly confronted with the Greatest Challenge of them all. What enables the hero to continue and to succeed? Consider Frodo in *Lord of the Rings*, for example. Is it lack of fear that helps him carry on against impossible odds? No, it is simply courage.

Courage depends on willingness, commitment, and truth. In fact courage arises from these other qualities. At no point along his journey does Frodo ever consider giving up. His willingness and his commitment are absolute. Even when he has to drag himself, almost unconscious, up treacherous terrain, we never for an instant see him contemplate turning back. It is simply not an option.

To transcend avoidance and receive the gift of courage we need the decision to commit, no matter what. People who successfully complete the Wealth Journey do not consider other alternatives. They have no backdoor options. They do not run back home to Mum at the first sign of a setback. They don't go back to their day job. They confront whatever comes their way, and keep going. Perseverance is the root of courage.

To begin the Wealth Journey you must commit

- What are you willing to commit to, right now?
- How can you demonstrate this commitment in a tangible way?
- How can you ensure you continue to honour this commitment?

I was chatting to a friend the other day. She was telling me how she'd love to just loaf off at home. She runs a very successful business. Part of the way she honours her commitment to her Wealth Journey is by having a partner in business. The partner's presence in her business ensures she gets in on time and delivers on her commitment to her business and Wealth Journey. She said having a partner is like having a lifeguard on the beach. 'I know how to swim,' she said, 'but the lifeguard is there, just in case.'

Sometimes we need help to deal with aspects of ourselves that are 'a work in progress'. This requires a great sense of humility, and self-knowledge. We can help ourselves by putting wealth checks and wealth guards in place to ensure we stay true to our course.

Wealth guard: *What can you put in place to help you keep on track at this point of your Wealth Journey?*

Okay, I can sense some of you are battling. I will give you another example. I have a lovely writing studio in Kalk Bay overlooking the harbour. One way I ensure I get there early to write each day is by dropping off the kids at school. This does not make any 'logical' sense at all, as I have to:

1. get up early which I do not like as I am not an early morning person;
2. drive in the opposite direction to my studio for about 20 minutes, then turn around and come back, past the house (!) and to the studio which is about three minutes away from home by car;
3. 'waste' about one hour of time as a result.

Also, Shaun's studio is halfway between school and home so it makes much more sense for him to drop off the kids, something which he did in fact do for many years.

But ... by doing what I do, I ensure I am writing by 8h30 or 8h45 each day. When I stay at home either to write in my study there, or to get ready to go to my studio later, I often get distracted, or land up reading a book, receiving email, chatting on the phone, dealing with domestic chores, having long soaks in the bath, or any one of a million other things – especially in winter. I am simply not as productive – no matter how I try to convince myself to the contrary! And please understand, that's despite the fact that I absolutely *love* writing!

So, find a way to keep yourself on your course. Here's that question again:

Wealth guard: *What can you put in place to help you keep on track at this point of your Wealth Journey?*

Cultivating the ability to Confront

Cultivating boldness and courage is a lifetime journey. Boldness, courage, means different things to different people. Some people are terrified of talking in front of a crowd. Yet these very same people may not have a problem rock climbing, or shark diving, or dressing wounds, or taking care of the infirm. Generally speaking, the more you face, the more you can face.

Without putting yourself in any physical or emotional danger, do some or all of the following this week, and repeat as often as possible:

- Say what you really want to say
- Do something you would not normally do
- Disagree with someone
- Complain about something in a restaurant and/or send your food back
- Say no
- Make that call
- Face someone you have been avoiding
- Don't back down
- Cry

'I will persist until I succeed, for that is the secret of success in all ventures'. I still remember these words from *The greatest salesman in the world* by Og Mandino.

Can you persist? Can you carry on and on and then on again, until you get the job done? Courage is born out of persistence. When you refuse to quit, when quitting is not even an option, when you are so firmly rooted in your purpose and intent that wild horses couldn't take you off course then courage will arise from deep within which will enable you to confront anything! This courage born out of perseverance is what will enable you to face the next challenge.

Ability to confront is the absolute cornerstone of wealth creation

2. Challenge : *Denial – Responsibility*
Key: *Truth*
Root: *Honour*

You have braved the forces of chaos and have persisted and persisted, building courage and the ability to confront. Now, your mind laughs and casts a little shadow of doubt on the proceedings. Either you begin to doubt, or others do it for you. They cite bad statistics, personal case scenarios or the economy. Perhaps you are tested in some trying way – something may not have gone according to plan. What do you do? Lay blame? Or take responsibility for what you are creating, and what you intend to create? Here, as at every level, you are being retested on the previous lesson and expanding on it. Can you really persist?

When we do not take responsibility, our power is diminished

The challenge of denial can emerge at any time, and can relate to not seeing what is really there, or to a distortion of truth.

Many times on our Wealth Journey, truth is brought into question. Do we walk the path of honour or do we follow the path of denial – not taking responsibility? These questions will mean something different for everyone.

Let's take a look at **DENIAL – RESPONSIBILITY**
(Write for 2 minutes on each)
- What do I deny as a general pattern in my life?
- What do I not take responsibility for?
- What do I take responsibility for?
- How do I deny responsibility for creating wealth?
- Which emotions arise when I refuse to take responsibility?
- What benefit do I get from denial?
- What do I deny, when it comes to money?
- Who/what do I blame/hold responsible for my wealth creation as a general pattern?
- How does denial impact on my wealth?
- What would I be doing if I knew I was the one totally responsible for creating my wealth?

Underline important words and phrases and summarise into one sentence.

Take any decisions you need to take as a result of this knowledge. Formulate a plan of action and do it. Make any changes you need to make in your life. Keep it simple. Keep it fun.

When we do not take responsibility, our power is diminished. When we are not talking and seeing truth, we are not walking our truth – which means we are off course. When we are off our course, we are no longer headed towards our destination.

Transcending DENIAL – *The gift of* TRUTH *through* HONOUR

Honour has become a really old fashioned word. As I am Greek, it was a word that featured strongly in my life from a very young age. Everything seemed to be 'honour' this and 'no honour' that. I learnt very early on, mostly through osmosis, that without honour, without a man's 'word' (being true) he is nothing. Death is a far more preferable option to the loss of honour, I was told.

As a parent I have learnt that children imitate what is shown rather than what is told. And this is true, for on the subject of honour and keeping one's word, my father lived his truth (if you'll excuse the pun). He associated only with those who also lived according to the principles of truth and honour. Somehow I took on this resonance, which I hope I am passing on to my children. It seems obvious and natural for me to flow with honour. I expect nothing less from myself than truth, no matter what the circumstances. For who or what is more important than my word, my truth, that I should want to bend it on their account? It is good to ask yourself this question.

But even though I was fortunate to be raised in such a resonance, I have also had to cultivate this quality for myself through the practice of delivering truth. It starts with the little things, and it's a form of training. You get better at it the more you do it. It also becomes easier the more you do it. Truth expands you. It helps you grow. And in time, it will pave your path with gold. Ultimately, a commitment to truth is a decision you take one day – it could be today. You simply decide to never again shrink your consciousness or to make less of yourself by denying truth – in speech, word, or deed.

So if you took the day off work to loaf around – admit it! If you promised your child something, deliver. And if you have been distorting some or other truth in your head to justify words or deeds that *you know* are not true – cut it out! Change it. Admit the truth – first to yourself, then to those who need to hear it.

As far as wealth creation is concerned, truth is one of your greatest weapons. You need to face where you are. Clearly know where you are going. Learn to see what is in front of you. Discover, as a result, what works and what does not. Be able to tell a good deal from a bad one. Choose the right people. All this cannot be done in denial. To have clear vision you need truth. To embrace truth you need to take responsibility.

If you can't tell the truth, then who can you believe?

Cultivating Truth and Honour

- What does truth mean to me?
- What does honour mean to me?
- Am I an honourable person?
- Am I a truthful person?
- How can I liberate the honour and truth within?
- How truthful am I in the wealth department?
- How honourable am I in my money dealings?
- What debts of honour remain unpaid?
- How can I reclaim my power by settling these debts?

How does it feel to always stand in my truth?

Take any decisions you need to take as a result of this knowledge. Formulate a plan of action and do it. Make any changes you need to make in your life. **Connect to the feel-good feeling.** *Keep it simple. Keep it light. Keep it fun.*

TAKE THE DECISION TO ALWAYS STAND
IN TRUTH AND HONOUR!
Honour your decision.

There is no more important or meaningful responsibility we can take than to be comfortable to stand, walk and speak our truth!

3. Challenge : *Struggle – Embrace*
Key: *Flow*
Root: *Allow*

This challenge emerges throughout The Wealth Journey™. It is our fundamental challenge in life as a whole – the ability to flow. All the books and theories and practices of being in the present, allowing what is, finding joy in the way things are, are based on transcending struggle and moving into flow.

By allowing, we are holding the space
of infinite possibility open

Struggle as a level of consciousness is quite deeply entrenched in most of the population, as I discussed before. Breaking free from its grasp is easy if you let go. That may sound strange and obvious but the whole problem with struggle is that we tense up and fight, even when we are trying to embrace. To embrace, though, we first need to open up our arms and our hearts. We need to allow. We need to pause – like the point between the in and the out breath. And that's where the trust and faith and believing in the impossible comes in. Because by allowing, we are holding the space of infinite possibility open, in full knowledge and confidence that what we want is on its way.

Let's take a look at **STRUGGLE – EMBRACE**
(Write for 2 minutes on each)
- What do I struggle with as a general pattern in my life?
- How does wealth-struggle manifest in my life?
- Which aspects of wealth creation do I struggle with?
- What beliefs underpin my need to struggle?
- What emotions arise when I struggle?
- When did my struggle begin?
- How do I embrace?
- What/who embraces me?
- How does struggle impact on my wealth?
- How can I embrace wealth? How can I allow wealth to embrace me?

Underline important words and phrases and summarise into one sentence.

Take any decisions you need to take as a result of this knowledge. Formulate a plan of action and do it. Make any changes you need to make in your life. Keep it simple. Keep it light. Keep it fun.

Transcending STRUGGLE – *The gift of* FLOW *through* ALLOWING

Many possibilities for wealth creation will come your way. Many doors will open. Many clues will present themselves, often cloaked. An innocuous comment, an offhand invitation could be the answer to your prayers, if you but knew it. Think back on your life and observe how one single event, usually quite insignificant, sets up a long series of connections, meetings and occurrences that changed life as you knew it, a few years down the line.

To take advantage of life's many opportunities you must allow yourself to flow. Believe that help is all around you, then open up to receiving it. Learning to flow is a practice. Depending on your temperament and life challenges you may find it easier to flow than others.

Flowing is not a totally passive undertaking. Flowing requires skill, elegance and grace. It requires presence and attention. Consider dancing, fencing (of the sword kind), t'ai-chi, walking with mindfulness. Consider breathing, or meditating. Consider singing. Consider stillness. They are all different expressions of flow.

> Flow can be found in anything which is done with such proficiency, such consummate skill as to seem effortless

Flow requires patience. It is the gift of allowing what is there to unfold.

Cultivating Flow

Depending on your preference, and what resonates with you, do some of the following:
- Take up dancing (preferably as a couple), t'ai-chi, aikido, fencing, meditation, rowing, sailing
- Walk with mindfulness and attention for 20 minutes each day
- Allow something you would not normally allow
- Sit next to a river and observe its flow
- Wait
- Listen
- Pay attention
- Wait (yes, again)

- Observe the breath as it enters and leaves your nostrils for 5 minutes daily in a quiet space
- Sit quietly with no distractions for 5-10 minutes daily
- Look for clues, signals, miracles, wonders; record your dreams
- Believe

While we struggle and deny we are closing off vital life and wealth force which cannot flow unimpeded through our lives. As we let go, embrace, and flow, we find that things effortlessly fall into place, amazing coincidences occur, the right people appear, our plans materialise. The gift of flow is what true luck is all about!

4. Challenge : *Control – Expand*
Key: *Generosity*
Root: *Openness*

I want to remind you once again (dear reader) of the holographic nature of this model. Each challenge can occur anywhere along the Wealth Consciousness scale. The challenges are like interwoven spirals, spreading out and then in, like a breath. So it is natural then, that having dealt with flow and allowing, we would now be faced with the challenge of control.

It's as if we need to grapple with this issue on a deeper level, learning the subtleties of presence, of real containment, of what it is to consciously create while allowing, so that our creation seems almost magical, incidental, miraculous. That's alchemy!

When we start to allow and to flow, we become afraid (that the tide may wash us away). Suddenly we are in the midst of a powerful current. We can feel its strength and we know we cannot fight or resist it, even as it flows towards the destination we ourselves have chosen. Yet we want to have some control over it. We want to direct it. We want to feel we are in charge. Try this on a real river with a real current and you will understand what I am saying.

> The gift of flow is what true luck is all about!

In the money making world, it is when everything is going great, all according to plan, no effort, no problem, it's happening (almost without you), so you try to Do Something – you interfere, you try to get involved in the process, you want to show that it's you who is doing it – and you blow it! Suddenly everything un-happens! Ever had this experience?

And the problem is fear, because deep down inside you start to doubt. Your mind says, 'Wait a minute, this is too easy, there's been no struggle (*refer to the previous section*), it can't be this simple! Do something for heaven's sake, before it all falls apart!' And so you get busy – you redo a proposal, or you call up the buyer to resell them on what they were sold on already and peeve them off, or you take some arbitrary action that has negative consequences.

What you are trying to do is pull the thing in, you're trying to control. And it's really the ego that's the culprit here because it wants to feel in charge.

Let's take a look at **CONTROL – EXPAND**
(Write for 2 minutes on each)
- How do I try to control? My life? Others? My wealth? (do each individually)
- Where does my control slip/get 'out of control'?
- What am I really trying to control?

- How does my need to control shrink me and my life?
- What feelings arise when I try to control?
- What emotions am I trying to ignore through controlling?
- Which areas of my life can I let go control of?
- What would happen if I 'lost control'?
- How can I expand? My life? Myself? My wealth?

Underline important words and phrases and summarise into one sentence.

Take any decisions you need to take as a result of this knowledge. Formulate a plan of action and do it. Make any changes you need to make in your life. Keep it simple. Keep it light. Keep it fun.

Transcending CONTROL – *the gift of* GENEROSITY *through* OPENNESS

I think it's time for a story ...

Once upon a time in a land far, far away, there lived a large magnificent octopus (well, really, that's what emerged when I started writing – a storyteller never questions who appears in a story). The octopus had long magnificent arms with fabulous suckers that shimmered pink and violet by the light of the moon.

Ethel, for that was the octopus's name, was a very capable octopus and she kept her home spick and span, prepared food, tended the coral garden, practised the violin, and manicured her suckers (keeping them clear of seaweed and fungus) *all at once*. Well, she had eight arms, you see. Every day, it was the same thing. Each tentacle had its job to do and she controlled them all. No slacking was allowed.

But, alas, Ethel wanted to travel the world. She wanted to see the Great Barrier Reef, she wanted to visit the Titanic, and even (she sometimes allowed herself to dream) find a mate. However, her work was never done and never a tentacle could be spared for enjoyment.

Now her neighbour was Eddie the crab and he was a lazy old fella, scuttling from place to place with never a worry, it would seem.

'You need to let go your tentacles, Ethel,' he would say. 'Open up your horizons. You can't control everything. Let the tides do their work. They will clear out your cave, and refresh your suckers too. Just give yourself up to the current. And, look, the little creatures will keep your garden clean if you will let them. Let go, Ethel and you will find what your heart desires.'

But Ethel never could. She would not trust the currents or the tides. And she looked askance at the scruffy little creatures who would nibble at her garden (keeping it clean, yes, but then she would have to share it).

Now, one day a terrible storm blew through the waters. It was sudden, it was the middle of the night when Ethel was taken up by the current and flung out of her cave into the waters below. The tides took her and shook her. They spun her and *shlupped* her. And when she uncurled the tentacles wrapped around her face, her familiar surroundings were gone. The current was strong and the tides still swirled around her, with ne'er a cave in sight.

Long trails of colourful fish giggled by; pilchards converged into balls before being swept away; langoustine seemed to be flying over her head. She remembered Eddie the crab's words – 'you need to let go your tentacles, Ethel', he'd said. And suddenly Ethel did. Just like that. In the blink of a moment. Besides, the effort of resisting the current suddenly seemed too great.

At first Ethel panicked, the feeling was so unfamiliar. But then, as she allowed herself to ride the current, she realised that it had many streams, each going in a different direction. She realised that, indeed, she could decide on a direction and the current would take her there much more quickly and easily than she could have ever done herself.

Home is where she was headed. She selected a current, allowed the flow to take her, and in no time at all she was back at her cave. There she found to her surprise that the cave had been swept clean by the tides. Her garden too looked fabulous, and the little creatures now living there peeped shyly at her from behind the rocks.

The next few days were uneventful. She officially welcomed the creatures into her garden, fiddled about a bit with her violin, but then there was little left to do. Everything around Ethel flowed effortlessly even while her tentacles remained unoccupied. And it was then that she remembered her mission. She wanted to travel! She wanted to go to The Great Barrier Reef! And now she knew what she had to do!

Ethel rose early the next day, selected a current and positioned herself in the path of the tide. Then she leaned back, she relaxed, and keeping the image of The Great Barrier Reef clearly in her mind, Ethel let her tentacles go, knowing that the current would take her there.

The End

The ability to Flow is not a totally passive undertaking
Flowing requires skill, elegance and grace. It requires presence
and attention

Cultivating Openness

Openness and expansion are linked. To create meaningful expansion you need to let go of control. If you look at any large organisation it will be obvious that at some point the owner had to place control in other hands in order to expand further.

Those who cannot or are unwilling to share control do not flourish. You cannot do everything yourself. In order to really grow, you need the help of others. Receiving help is only possible if you are open. Sharing control is only possible if you practise generosity. Openness and generosity need to be cultivated, like anything else.

Depending on your preference, and what resonates with you, do some (or all) of the following:

- Open your heart to someone (it could be a stranger) and tell them how you really feel
- Drop off your old magazines at the hospital and visit the sick
- Visit an old persons' home and chat with someone
- Hold the hand of someone who's dying
- Watch a really sad movie – allow yourself to cry
- Embrace the next really different idea that comes your way
- Jump at the next opportunity
- Tell someone you love them

When you open yourself up to the flow of money,
the flow of money will simply flow towards you

5. Challenge : *Complicate – Simplify*
Key: *Choice*
Root: *Knowledge*

This challenge is what is being grappled with in the Co-Dependence level of Wealth Consciousness. Now, there is a choice of making things really complicated, or simplifying them. And this decision will set the tone and direction for all the levels of Wealth Consciousness that follow – from Independence right up to Affluence.

This choice and challenge is a profoundly personal one too, as you are now beginning to contemplate a picture of yourself and of the future that expands beyond mere survival. Here you are asking yourself 'what's it all about?', and 'what do I really need and want?'

Keep it Simple ...

This challenge stands at the midpoint between the first four and the last four levels of Wealth Consciousness. It is a point of pause, of consolidation, of the space between the in and out breath. Here, as you are about to launch into Independence, you have a good sense of what is possible. You are no longer as afraid of the future as you once were. Now you know, with a great degree of certainty, that you can do it, that it is possible. And now you pause to ask yourself some big questions, to reassess your destination, and sometimes to completely redesign it.

Or you may lose (part of) the plot by getting busy. You do not take the pause, you do not see it. You do not realise you have a choice, you do not become informed enough, you lack the knowledge, (either of self, or of your situation) with which to make a well-considered decision.

So you invite and cultivate more debt, expenditure, expansion. (Remember we have just embraced expansion in the previous challenge. Now you are retested in this area, to ensure your expansion is grounded.)

Here is an extreme example of what I mean. Complication in all its glory is shown under Enron Venture Capitalism. Bit of a long way to make a point, but some of this is really very good! And it's time for a funny break too!

Socialism
You have two cows.
You give one to your neighbour.

Communism
You have two cows.
The State takes both and gives you some milk.

Fascism
You have two cows.
The State takes both and sells you some milk.

Nazism
You have two cows.
The State takes both and shoots you.

Bureaucratism
You have two cows.
The State takes both, shoots one, milks the other, and then throws the milk away ...

Traditional Capitalism
You have two cows. You sell one and buy a bull.
Your herd multiplies, and the economy grows. You sell them and retire on the income.

Surrealism
You have two giraffes.
The government requires you to take harmonica lessons.

An American Corporation
You have two cows.
You sell one, and force the other to produce the milk of four cows.
Later, you hire a consultant to analyse why the cow has dropped dead.

Enron Venture Capitalism
You have two cows.
You sell three of them to your publicly listed company, using letters of credit opened by your brother-in-law at the bank, then execute a debt/equity swap with an associated general offer so that you get all four cows back, with a tax exemption for five cows. The milk rights of the six cows are transferred via an intermediary to a Cayman Island Company secretly owned by the majority shareholder who sells the rights to all seven cows back to your listed company. The annual report says the company owns eight cows, with an option on one more. You sell one cow to buy a new president of the United States, leaving you with nine cows. No balance sheet provided with the release. The public then buys your bull.

(Keep it Simple!)

A Japanese Corporation

You have two cows.

You redesign them so they are one-tenth the size of an ordinary cow and produce twenty times the milk. You then create a clever cow cartoon image called 'Cowkimon' and market it worldwide.

A German Corporation

You have two cows.

You re-engineer them so they live for a hundred years, eat once a month, and milk themselves.

An Italian Corporation

You have two cows, but you don't know where they are. You decide to have lunch.

A Russian Corporation

You have two cows.

You count them and learn you have five cows.

You count them again and learn you have four cows.

You count them again and learn you have two cows.

You stop counting cows and open another bottle of vodka.

A Swiss Corporation

You have 5000 cows. None of them belong to you. You charge the owners for storing them.

An Indian Corporation

You have two cows.

You worship them.

A British Corporation
You have two cows.
Both are mad.

An Australian Corporation
You have two cows.
Business seems pretty good.
You close the office and go for a few beers to celebrate.

A New Zealand Corporation
You have two cows.
The one on the left looks very attractive ...

Okay, where were we? We were looking at Complication. I have seen many a business or marketing proposal that is as baffling as the Enron example. The element of dishonesty may have been missing, but the confusion and 'complexity' was certainly there.

To simplify means to focus

Does your life or wealth look a bit like that example or does it seem to be heading that way? Perhaps it's time to reassess your options. This challenge also relates to becoming informed. Here you may have started to, or be on the brink of starting to, acquire some spare cash. What will you do with it? How will you invest it? Perhaps as a result of transcending the previous challenge you are looking at expanding your business? You may be considering giving up some of the control to others. What will that involve? How best to do it? What structures do you require in place? But most importantly 'where are you headed now?'

That's what the Simplify is all about. Also, it's about making space for the new. Throwing out what no longer serves, and keeping the space open for the new to arrive, without introducing new clutter and complication. To simplify is to focus.

When you truly understand something, when you are really clear on what it means, you are able to explain it in its simplest form to anyone, even a young child. Complication is the result of incomplete trains of thought, unclarified assumptions, unsubstantiated conclusions, inability to construct an argument, sometimes untruths, and lack of direction and focus! Complication is not a sign of intelligence. Nor is it a sign of lack of intelligence or education not to understand convoluted complication. Complication in a document is a sign that something is being hidden – there is something that is not being revealed – sometimes not even to the creator of the document. Perhaps the complication is masking the real intention or beliefs or attitudes of the author. Perhaps it is more sinister than that. Ouch, but she can be testy, this one!

Make sure you understand anything you sign your name to. Sure, landlords are not used to people reading the lease agreement, let alone questioning or modifying the clauses. But whose problem is that? Double ouch!

Also, as I have said elsewhere in my books, make sure your investment consultant, or new business partner, or company you are investing your hard-earned money into, can explain to you quite clearly, so that you can understand quite clearly:

    ~ what you are getting yourself into
    ~ how it works ('too complicated to explain' does not cut it!)
    ~ what it's costing you
    ~ how much the other party earns (in the case of a third party)

~ what returns you can expect

~ what the risks are – in other words, what can go wrong

~ how you get out of the agreement

~ what track record/referrals are available on the people/ product you are dealing with

~ what happens in the worst case scenario

~ what happens if you need to get out of the investment in a hurry

If they cannot, or will not give you the answers to these questions, move on. This is good advice. If you cannot face asking any of these questions go back to the section on Confront.

Do not invest or become financially involved in anything, unless you have the balls and nerve and confidence not only to ask these questions, but to know deep down inside that you are fully entitled and justified to do so! Did I say this is really good advice?

Let's take a look at **COMPLICATE – SIMPLIFY**
(Write for 2 minutes on each)

- How complicated is my life? My money dealings? (do each individually)
- What don't I know about my business? My life? My wealth? My investments?
- What am I in the dark about in my life?
- Where can I turn for information/help/clarity?
- What do I need to know? Make a list
- What do I avoid looking at by creating complication where there is none?
- What is simple?
- What can I rely upon?

Take any decisions you need to take as a result of this knowledge. Formulate a plan of action and do it. Make any changes you need to make in your life. Keep it simple. Keep it light. Keep it fun.

Keep it Simple!

Transcending COMPLICATION – *the gift of* CHOICE *through* KNOWLEDGE

As those of you who have worked with me can attest to, I am a disciple of simplicity.

I believe there is always a better and simpler way to do anything. But simplicity cannot be fully exercised without Choice. This is not just a truism. Choice cannot be exercised without knowledge – which I have covered at length above.

Apart from knowledge of external matters, we also need internal knowledge – self-knowledge. That is what we are trying to acquire through the various transformational processes we engage in. It is a lifetime journey. When we move from complication to simplification, we engage in the process of trimming off the fat of our internal lives, letting go what no longer serves, and also cutting to the core of what is really meaningful and important to us. We complicate to hide, to avoid issues, to distract ourselves from what really matters, from what we should be looking at. To simplify means to see what is there.

Simplification on the personal level means moving through the superficiality of our personalities and baggage and ego to the innermost part of our being – the part that is who we truly are and, more importantly, who we aspire to become. When we know this, real choices can be made. We are no longer being swept along with the circumstances of our lives, we are consciously choosing our direction. And this is usually quite simple.

Cultivating Simplicity

- How can I simplify my life?
- What are the three most important things in my life?
- What do I want to pour my energy into daily?
- What is the most important thing I can be doing with my time?
- What do I yearn for?
- How can I get what I yearn for? List 8 steps
- What do I choose to do with my life? With my wealth?
- What can I let go of?
- What does simplicity mean to me?

How does it feel to live a clear and simple life?

Take any decisions you need to take as a result of this knowledge. Formulate a plan of action and do it. **Connect with the feel-good feeling.** *Make any changes you need to make in your life. Keep it simple. Keep it light. Keep it fun.*

Keep it (Really) Simple!

6. Challenge : *Dissipate – Contain*
Key: *Purpose*
Root: *Service*

This challenge corresponds with the first level of real wealth on our Wealth Consciousness scale – that of Independence. Now you have money! Well Done! And on the topic of this challenge, containment, I have written a whole book, *The Money Well*™ – *How to Contain Wealth*! Get a copy if you don't have one, and work through the processes in it.

In the previous challenge we looked at simplifying, getting to the core of things, finding out what really matters, what you really want. Here, in this challenge, this is tested in a big way. You have money. What will you do with it? How will you contain it? For if you don't contain money, it will most surely drain away.

I will not spend too much time discussing containment – you really do need to read *The Money Well*™ for that. It works with the metaphor of a container – how you need one, what it is made of, and how to overcome obstacles to containment and to money flow. Simply put, you need a clear and specific goal or destination and, more accurately, the feeling of a new beingness for wealth to flow towards. To contain wealth you need a container. To contain more wealth you need a bigger container. Survival will no longer be enough.

So the challenge here is to contain, versus scatter or waste or dissipate, and the key to that is service. Now service does not need to be some heroic, altruistic mission of charity – though that would be nice. Service is a resonance, it is a frequency. It is delivery. It is often about putting the needs of others before your own. It is definitely putting the needs of the greater good first. And that takes us back to the previous challenge – because the greater good is also part of your innermost desires.

Which brings us to purpose, which is key. It is The Key. But purpose too need not be this profound revelation acquired after wrestling with bears on a vision quest in the Rockies. Purpose can be very simple. Purpose is pure simplicity itself. And when you think about it, we all have pretty simple service to deliver in day-to-day life which we often neglect in favour of grandiose and more 'meaningful' endeavours.

As mothers and fathers our purpose is to hold a space for our children to flourish and prosper, to feel safe in the world, to grow into healthy and balanced human beings. What can be nobler than that? As beings on this planet our purpose is to learn how to be human. As friends, our purpose is to support; as partners, to love and cherish; as workers to create; as teachers to learn. This is how we can serve our highest potential. This is how we can be of service to ourselves and to humanity as a whole.

> Recognising and connecting with our purpose
> enables us to contain both our lives and our wealth

Let's take a look at **DISSIPATE – CONTAIN**
(Write for 2 minutes on each)
- What/who drains my resources?
- Where do I waste time/money/opportunity/energy? (do each one separately)
- How do I contain my life/wealth/precious possessions?
- What is my purpose in my various roles?
- Where/how can I better serve?
- What is my greater purpose?
- How can I fulfil it?
- What do I need to do to align myself with my purpose?

How does it feel to be aligned with my purpose?

*Take any decisions you need to take as a result of this knowledge. Formulate a plan of action and do it. **Connect with the feel-good feeling!** Make any changes you need to make in your life. Keep it simple. Keep it light. Keep it fun.*

Transcending DISSIPATION – *the gift of* PURPOSE *through* SERVICE

I have always been drawn by tales of 'the ordinary man'. Like the Buddhist idea of 'before enlightenment draw water, after enlightenment draw water'. Like the Taoist notion that in the ordinary lies the extraordinary, that it is extraordinary and noble to live a good and ordinary life.

In the west at this time we seem obsessed with the notion of 'our purpose'. Finding our purpose, finding our passion, living the life we were meant to live, finding the work we love. And in this quest we lose the poignancy of living the simplicity of the moment. It is no longer enough for a mother to master the art of motherhood; for a father to be a good father, provider and husband; for children to enjoy being children through fun and play.

I remember in the early years of becoming a mother I felt lost, I did not know what to do. I could not decide between teacher and writer and healer. I could not decide if I should go back into business. I thought I had lost my purpose. I said, 'I don't know what I'm meant to be doing any more.' A friend replied, 'What if you are meant to just be a mother? What if your greatest job is to be the best mother you can be to these children?' Well, I was stumped! I still am, when I really connect with that question!

There is no greater purpose than simply doing
what is there to be done

We can be of service whatever we are doing. And when we approach whatever we are doing with the attitude of service, then our purpose becomes revealed. Recently, the same wise friend told me, 'Sometimes it's as you start doing things, that your goal is revealed.'

To simply do what is there to be done is the greatest purpose and service we can offer the world and ourselves. It is also the secret to contentment. And when we are content, then we contain, which is the subject of this challenge.

Cultivating Containment

- Think back to a time when you felt content. Connect with that feeling
- Think of another time you felt content. Connect with that feeling
- List the things/situations/components you need for contentment
- Decide on exactly what you would do if money was not an issue
- Accurately describe how you will contain your next million
- Create containers for your talents, aspirations, fun, service
- Create a container for the new wealthy you that you are moving towards becoming

How does it feel to be content?

*Take any decisions you need to take as a result of this knowledge. Formulate a plan of action and do it. **Connect with the feel-good feeling!** Make any changes you need to make in your life. Keep it simple. Keep it light. Keep it fun.*

Your purpose is the greatest container you will ever have for your wealth. Cultivating contentment is an important component of containment, for in essence you can only contain what you are comfortable and content to contain.

Creating a container for your talents could mean setting aside time to bake, or taking up golf or dancing. Creating a container for fun could mean setting time aside each week to party, or go out for a romantic dinner, or to laugh and be silly. Creating a container for your aspirations could mean taking a class in yachting – even though you may seem miles away from owning one. Creating a container for the new wealthy you could mean going on a diet, trying on some really expensive clothes or shoes, or taking a private jet on a test flight.

What you want to take away from these experiences, most of all, is the feeling! Store it away so you can access it at will. And continue to practise! To have more wealth you need to be able to contain more wealth.

Your purpose is the container for your wealth

7. Challenge: *Daydream – Create*
Key: *Action*
Root: *Grounding*

On the Wealth Consciousness levels you have arrived at Comfort. Although this challenge, like all the others, may find you at any level, it is in Comfort where it's the most dangerous as it is here that you have the most to lose. As always, this challenge is a retest of the previous challenge, for once you have got some semblance of containment going, the lure of sitting back and daydreaming instead of grounding your gains with action, will be very great.

The challenge of Daydream – Create is also very apparent on the first few levels of Wealth Consciousness – in Ignorance, when we are battling to persevere, and in Blame, when we struggle to take responsibility, the temptation to take refuge in daydreaming is very strong.

Instead of doing something, we may sit and build castles in the air. We may discuss what we will do once the money comes in, or when an investor backs our invention. And although these are very necessary starting points in the Wealth Journey, there soon comes the time of action – which is the key and gift of this challenge.

In fact (take careful note of this), Action is the way forward on most levels of consciousness – except for Struggle and Dependence where you need to cultivate flow which is another form of action to the one we are talking about here. Action is also the way through most challenges (again, with the exception of the two just mentioned).

When we reach Comfort, we may feel we have arrived, it will certainly feel like it. It is the start of knowing we are wealthy, we have successfully created, we have overcome many obstacles to get here, we can now enjoy the fruits of our labour ... or so we think. But ...

... this is only the start. In reality we are only at the start of the wealth creation line. In reality the steps leading up to this point were preparation. It is very dangerous to pause here. Pausing here is like being lulled by the sirens towards the rocks. Staying here is like becoming stuck in one of the demi-god realms, where, according to some models of consciousness, everything is so fantastic that you lose the plot, you forget about enlightenment, and usually crash all the way down to one of the hell realms. (Do I have your attention?) This model may be taken literally or metaphorically, depending on your viewpoint – certainly we see evidence of such activities right here on planet earth.

Now you may say to me, wait a minute, did I not just go

through overcoming the previous challenge through creating a container? And that is just the point. As you have seen, each challenge overcome has to be grounded and integrated in the next challenge. And even as you create a container to contain, so you must be looking to ground that container with action.

Ground your wealth with action

So here, at this challenge, we are looking at grounding your gains. We are looking at transcending Daydreaming through Create. We are looking at Action. You are here, feeling okay, things are running smoothly. What will you do next? Where do you go from here? Because unless you do something – life, wealth, and what you have created, will spiral back to where it was before you started your journey. This is called the beta decay force, entropy – a scientific phenomenon that says: if left alone (or more exactly, if no creation is being continued), things will break down and decay and fall apart. We have evidence of this in our own bodies. We see it around in nature, which is ever abundant, ever creating, always ending one cycle with the beginning of another.

Consider, also, that you have built momentum. Unless you use it to move on, you will lose it. Fast. You need to move, you need to act. You need to ground or consolidate what you have achieved. You need to integrate, absorb, before you get indigestion. Have I used enough metaphors here?

Bear in mind that even though some of you reading this book are familiar with this space and challenge, while others may not yet be here, this challenge can come to you at any point along your Wealth Journey, so it is good to know how to transcend it.

Let's take a look at **DAYDREAM – CREATE**
(Write for 2 minutes on each)
- What are my recurring daydreams/fantasies about? Make a list
- Which of these have been with me the longest? Mark them
- Which of these do I want to let go of? Cross them out
- Are there any other dreams, aspirations I want to add to the list? Add them
- What can I do now that I could not do before?
- Which of these dreams do I want to commit to turning into reality?

How does it feel to be the (co-)creator of these new realities?

*Take any decisions you need to take as a result of this knowledge. Formulate a plan of action and do it. **Connect with the feel-good feeling!** Make any changes you need to make in your life. Keep it simple. Keep it light. Keep it fun.*

Transcending DAYDREAMING – *the gift of* ACTION *through* GROUNDING

It may seem that through action you acquire grounding, but I believe that it is the grounding that provides the impetus for action, in the same way that in a tree it is the roots that make it possible for the tree and branches and leaves to grow. Grounding and action are two sides of the same coin. New gains have to be grounded.

The level of Comfort has to be owned, embraced, absorbed – in other words, grounded. You need to cultivate your ability to have more. This is done through containment – making sure that as you grow, so you expand your container. It is done through grounding – planting long strong roots from which your next creation will grow. And it is also done through action, which means create!

This challenge invites you to create a new reality. To use the platform you are on as a launching pad for your next level – in this case Wealth. You have to create the roots from which your new reality will flow. You need to accommodate and develop the new you that you are becoming. You have to keep going.

This is also the challenge you need to integrate any time you are changing track, getting a new job, or going into a new sphere of activity. Any time you are expanding into a new space you need to ensure that firstly you create a bigger container to accommodate the additional wealth and the expanded new you, and then that you ground your new state through inspired action.

What does that mean – in 'reality'... ? Well, it means that when, as a writer, I come to end of writing my first book and get it published (Hooray!), I do not get all complacent and think 'This is it – I have arrived,' but I continue writing. I continue to write because that's what writers do. I continue to write because I have built up momentum for writing and I don't want to lose it. I write because one needs to give to receive – in other words, outflow equals inflow. I write because the readers need the next book. I write because I want my books to sell. I write because I need to keep creating. I write because I need to get from Comfort to Wealth in terms of being a writer.

You can substitute 'writing' in the example above with art, consulting, business, marketing, as well as anything else you can think of, and the activity required, as well as the results to be created, will remain the same.

The exact steps for consciously creating a new reality are in my book *The Art of Conscious Creation*™ (which I will write soon), and which has to be read together with *The Money Well*™. Here we are looking at grounding and action. In the reflection below, you will have the opportunity to ground the process of creation through some very powerful acts.

Cultivating Creation

- Celebrate where you are at this time
- Appreciate all that you have achieved – make a list
- Connect with the feeling of wealth and abundance
- Reflect upon and celebrate your good fortune
- Make a list of all the things you are grateful for in your life
- Take ownership of where and who you are at the moment
- Do anything you need to do to help you take ownership
- Take the pool of all that feel-good feeling and project it across time into your new dream
- See yourself in the new picture
- Act!

Take any decisions you need to take as a result of this knowledge. Formulate a plan of action and do it. **Connect with the feel-good feeling!** *Make any changes you need to make in your life. Keep it simple. Keep it light. Keep it fun.*

Taking ownership means absorbing, integrating, becoming a part of your new space in your Wealth Journey. Often, physical changes can help us to consolidate inner transformation. For example, when I first owned a fund management company, I was still driving an old VW Beetle. One day my business partner said, 'You know you are now The Director of a registered financial institution, you cannot go around in an old Beetle.' Naturally, I protested and kicked up my heels (we resist change ...). But he was right and I got a BMW – clichéd I know, but it helped me in the long run to grow into the new me I was becoming. You may need to rethink your wardrobe, or some small detail of it. Perhaps you need a new hairdo. You may need to ditch your surfing outfit, or your beard, or your tie-dye T-shirts.

You have to create the roots from which your new reality will flow

You may also need to adopt some attitude (which I believe one should have in good measure in any case) which befits your new position. Here's a question to ask yourself in any situation. If I were Rockefeller (or Branson, or Oppenheimer), how would I deal with this situation? What would I demand of it? What would I expect of the world and, most importantly of all, how would or could this person/organisation be dealing with me and this situation?

In other words, begin to believe that what's good enough for Rockefeller is definitely good enough for you. Moreover, expect this from the world, and the world will deliver. For example: If you were Rockefeller would you get a table at that restaurant? At the last minute? No matter how full? If you were Branson, would the garage expect you to take your car in for its service or would they collect? Would they gladly make a courtesy car available? (Never mind whether Branson has a chauffeur and doesn't need a courtesy car.) So ... if the garage or restaurant (or whatever) can do it (for whoever), it means they can do it – for you. Not so? You'd absolutely better believe it!

You may think I am helping you to cultivate arrogance and elitism. And heck, let's face it, there's nothing wrong with that ... we all need to embrace the arrogant side of ourselves that says 'Yes, I am worth this'; the elitist side of our nature that says, 'I can be a cut above where I am now'. But, what I am actually hoping, however, is that you will realise that anything, and everything is possible – for this is the key to creation.

I am also hoping you will transcend any feelings you may be holding of being small, apologetic, less than, afraid of, and take up your power. So walk in to that restaurant at peak hour and expect the *maitre d'* to find you a table! Do it just for fun. He will.

The key is just to stand there and smile sweetly when he says 'It's full'. That is called 'holding the space of possibility open'. Just wait. Smile. Say nothing. (I did this on Valentine's Eve once – great fun!) Wait. Believe. Wait. Finally (shaking his head in bemusement, puzzlement and plain downright confoundment, which literally translated means: *I-have-no-idea-why-I-am-about-to-do-what-I-am-about-to-do*), the *maitre d'* will lead you to a cosy table (which was there all along, probably waiting for some important person like yourself to make it appear). Try it!

Then celebrate! Regularly ground your gains by reflecting on your good fortune. Take ownership of what you have, and what you have achieved, and project these good feeling into a new you in the future. Be grateful for what you've got! And watch it grow!

8. Challenge : *Dictate – Direct*
Key: *Vision*
Root: *Clarity*

Wealth is fantabulous!

You have arrived at WEALTH! You are wealthy and you know it! And of course you cannot fail to notice how cultivating a cool stare in that restaurant was fabulous preparation for this challenge of Dictate – Direct. Yes, if you're wealthy and you know it, clap your hands ... I think I must write a poem to celebrate! My editor Maire is always disappointed if I don't write at least one poem in every book. Maire is pronounced Moira, by the way, for those who have been wondering.

> Wealth rhymes with health –
> what more could you need?
> Wealth is so wonderful, all worries recede.

> We hope not your hairline though – that could be tough
> but use some cash for a transplant –
> you'll have more than enough!

> (This poem is not clear, it has no direction –
> it's a scattered page waster
> and needs some correction.)

> But you cannot Avoid it; you must Persevere,
> with Courage, Confront
> that which you fear.

> You cannot Deny; you need to Accept

that Honour and Truth
are Responsibly kept

and then transcend Struggle,
Embrace, Flow, Allow;
go with the moment; stay in the now.

Expand, don't Control,
be Generous, be Open,
and soon all will come, just as you were hoping.

Don't Complicate; Simplify,
use Knowledge, use Choice,
and soon Independence will make you rejoice.

Use Purpose and Service
to help you Contain
or everything Dissipates clear down the drain.

Don't Daydream! Don't Daydream! Don't Daydream!
Create!
Take Action to Ground your gains!
Don't sit and wait!

Then Wealth will appear,
as if out of the blue –
Clarity and Vision will now help you through.

Direct, don't Dictate,
and you will gain Power.
Stand straight and accept it; there's no need to cower!

Fuelled by Gratitude
you'll reach higher and higher
your Divine Connection to help you aspire

to dizzying heights,
ahead of the throng,
until with a flourish, you will finish this song

(in the back of a Cadillac, or on top of a yak.
You can have what you want
Now how about that?) . . .

Wealth is fantabulous!
Wealth is enormous!
Wealth is an energy, powerful and formless!
(Repeat)

And now, dear reader,
I had better return
To the eighth Wealth Challenge, where you will soon
learn . . .

. . . that the thing to avoid most in Wealth is Seriousness! I believe many a person has lost (or never made) their fortune because they took money, and themselves, too seriously. Wealth, as I explained in my first book, *Money Alchemy* ™ – *into wealth and beyond* (will the ads never end?!), is a light and magical energy. When you stop playing, when you make things heavy and solid, the flow of wealth energy is interrupted. It can no longer flow.

Wealth is enormous

This may sound a bit contradictory of the advice I gave you in the previous challenge, where I was getting you to take ownership of the new wealthy you through grounding, but it is not. First a tree must grow big, strong, firm roots and a base (bark and branches), then light gentle foliage can dance in the wind.

Quite aptly, the challenge we face in Wealth is Dictate which we need to transform through Vision with Clarity creating Direct(ion) in order to move into the next and final challenge of Power. Abuse of power comes from not transcending the Dictate – Direct level of Wealth Consciousness.

At Wealth you have power, a lot of it. You can now make a difference. You can certainly get your table, get your car collected and much, much more. What do you do? How do you mediate this energy? How do you direct it? Because, energetically, at Wealth you are now (just about) controlling the equivalent of a nuclear station. I use this example, because the potential for both benefit and destruction with nuclear energy is very apparent. The same can be said for wealth, and there is a lot of responsibility that goes with both.

Wealth is an energy, powerful and formless

Dictate is a more extreme version of Control, which we encountered in the fourth challenge. We are in a sense revisiting this challenge at a higher, subtler, more powerful resonance – the eight being two fours, for those who are into numerology. Transforming Dictate into skilful Direct is an art.

It is easy to dictate with wealth, more subtle to direct. How we negotiate this challenge will set the tone for how we will deal with the next one – Power. Dictating, like controlling, eventually shrinks energy and creates a static – something that does not move. What we want and need is expansion, and a vision – a direct(ion) which will give clarity to our situation. We also need Action, we need to keep moving.

Let's take a look at **DICTATE – DIRECT**
(Write for 2 minutes on each)
- How do I try to impose my will on the world?
- What is my greatest fear?
- What am I trying to control?
- How am I containing what I have?
- How am I containing my potential?
- What potential exists in my future?
- What do I still want to do? Make a list
- What do I need to go to the next level?
- What dreams remain uncreated?
- What clarity do I need?
- How can I direct my life?
- What direction do I need?

How does it feel to have clear vision?

Take any decisions you need to take as a result of this knowledge. Formulate a plan of action and do it. **Connect with the feel-good feeling!** *Make any changes you need to make in your life. Keep it simple. Keep it light. Keep it fun.*

Transcending the need to DICTATE – the gift of VISION through CLARITY

Now is the time for a truly great and expansive vision. Now is the time to use your imagination to clearly see a wonderful future, some unique solutions for your company, country, or the world. Now is the time to get real Direction. Transcending this challenge is preparation for the next, where direction is almost totally internalised.

When we speak of direction we are talking of real flow arising from deep within. We are looking at a high degree of self-knowledge. At this point we know who we are, and have some idea of what we are here to do, if not all the details. Life around us is flowing quite smoothly, almost effortlessly. Our direction is done almost by remote control. It follows and is informed by our consciousness, our frame of mind, our resonance. This is a huge responsibility.

Our challenge is to get Clarity, refine, get Direction. And so we move backwards and forwards between Daydreaming, Creating, Grounding; and Clarifying and Directing our Vision, as we try to stabilise enough to move into Affluence and deal with the challenge of Power.

If we get into dictating, we may lose the plot. If we think, having arrived at Wealth, that all we now need to do is to protect what we have, guard it, ensure we do not lose or squander it, try to make certain it does not shrink or diminish – then we may be headed for a downward spiral. Water must continue to flow. If left to stagnate, it will spoil. It is the same with energy and with money (which is energy), and with life. It must move, it must flow, in order to grow.

Wealth
must flow
in order
to grow

Here's my first Live Wealth® bumper sticker: 'Wealth must flow in order to grow'! I hope by the time you read this book you may already have one on your car. Especially if you live in Tokyo and Düsseldorf, and Sydney! (You have one in New York too? That's fantastic!)

Contemplate the following in as much detail as possible:
- How can I ensure my wealth continues to flow?
- Which areas of my life are stagnating?
- How am I trying to dictate my wealth, my life?
- What do I need to do to skilfully direct my wealth?
- What solutions can I provide for the earth?
- What would I do if I was the president?
- Which path has opened up for me?
- Which signs and signals have appeared lately in my life?
- What is my vision?
- What greater purpose am I being nudged towards?
- What direction am I moving towards?

Wealth must flow in order to grow

Cultivating Direct(ion)

To cultivate direction we need clarity. Clarity is nothing more than seeing what is there without distortion created by untruths, denial, and ego. Clear direction is the knowledge of who you really are, and why you are here.

The following exercise is very useful. It is best to do it with a trusted friend. It creates profound and meaningful results. Sit facing your partner, very close, but not touching. Maintain full eye contact – especially the Questioner.

The questioner asks the question: *Who are you?*

You respond with whatever comes to mind, until you are silent. The questioner listens, holding the space. Then the questioner asks the question again, with full attention and intention. You respond again. Repeat for at least half an hour – maybe longer. Until you reach a real Aha! moment.

When you connect with who you really are, your own light will illuminate your Direction. It is out of this light that we hope to connect with and radiate our power, which is the next challenge.

9. Challenge : *Power – Transcend*
Key: *Appreciate*
Root: *Divine Connection*

This is the challenge of Affluence. It is the point at the end of the line. It is a death even as it is a new beginning. We need to rise like the phoenix from the ashes or we will surely die. In Power we have come full circle starting at the beginning once again.

When we arrive at this point, we know who we are and have a pretty clear idea of what we are here to do. Life around us is flowing smoothly, effortlessly. All our needs are taken care of. We are at a point of equilibrium, but now we need to rock the boat in order to move forward (which we may be loath to do). At Power and Affluence we direct by remote control. Our path follows and is informed by our consciousness, our frame of mind, our resonance. We create as we think. This is a huge responsibility.

When you connect with who you really are,
your own light will illuminate your direction

We are now aware (or are becoming aware) of the greater responsibility towards ourselves and the greater whole (whatever that may mean for each of us). And so, once again, and many times over, we have to face the full gamut of the wealth challenges, sometimes in the course of a day or a week. But this time, the move from challenge to challenge is not played out in the outside world, now the struggle is internal.

So even as a part of us knows we have arrived at the moment of greatest potential, we wrestle with ourselves. We go into Avoidance, we don't want to rock the boat, we don't want to move further. We don't want to confront the enormous potential of what we could be now accomplishing. And we have little external pressure to do so. We are fine. We are more than fine. We don't have to, or need to, do anything. We can loaf until the end of time – no one and nothing is there to stop us. Our direction at this level is (almost) completely self-created. We have autonomy. We have (almost) infinite and total choice.

We procrastinate for a while and then we may deny what we know, refusing to take responsibility. 'I cannot solve the earth's problems,' we may say: 'I cannot help to feed all the orphans, or save the sharks. I do not want to teach, or heal. It's too big a task. I have done enough. I am tired. I do not want to move into my full potential.' We fight and struggle against what we know to be the truth. We will not embrace the flow of the river which is drawing us into its current. We will not own up to our destiny.

Then, in the next breath, we pull ourselves together, open our hearts, expand, try to create a container, all excited at the prospect. Then we may lapse into daydreaming again and move between that and creating and grounding our vision which sometimes we can see with total clarity. That is the challenge of coming into Power and integrating it into Transcendence.

There are no questions to ask here, or if there are, you must create them. I cannot offer you guidance. Here, we need simply to listen to the quiet inner voice. No one is out there to offer input when you reach this point. You are (almost) alone.

Integrating *POWER into* TRANSCENDENCE *– the gift of* APPRECIATION *through* DIVINE CONNECTION

You probably noticed that whereas I have been talking of transcending challenges up to this point, now I am talking of integrating (in the heading). In fact the whole journey through the various challenges is a progressive integration of power. Integrating our power is what the Wealth Journey is actually all about.

Listen to the quiet inner voice

I must tell you the story of Tiger Woods. For those who may not know, he is the best golfer on the planet. Some time in his early twenties, at the height of his success, at the point when he was number one, Tiger Woods realised that although he was the best golfer in the world, if he was to become the best golfer of all time and the best golfer the world has ever known, he had to change his swing.

Now changing your swing is something that no golfer ever does. The very way he was playing his game was what was putting Tiger Woods at the top. Still he knew, deep down inside, that he had to change his swing. He had to let go of, and unlearn, and change, everything he knew that had made him successful up until this point. Can you imagine even thinking that? Goes right against the 'if it's working, don't mess with it' theory! Everyone around him was appalled. Everyone around him begged him to reconsider. But Tiger Woods held firm. Can you imagine that, too?

In the year that followed his decision, he fell out of top position, he earned no recognition or awards, and little money. But *then*, THEN ... he re-emerged, better, better, far better than he'd ever been before. And there seems little doubt that he will indeed be (indeed is) the best golfer the world has ever known.

Can you begin to imagine what it took to decide, let alone implement, such a choice? Can you imagine doing something like that? And do you know that the ability to do what he did, alone already marked him as the best.

That is what integrating power is all about!

Let's take our hats off to Tiger Woods!

(Okay, so when I first wrote this, it was a good year or two before Mr Woods was having his personal life publicly scrutinised – more importantly, he changed his swing a good decade before he was swinging. So let's leave it at that.)

We call the intense, deep, and profound inner conviction that (I imagine) Tiger Woods had, Divine guidance. And no matter what our concept of the Divine is, the ability to connect with, listen to, hear, understand, and act upon this connection can be seen as the pinnacle of personal power.

All right, I see quite a few of you are huffing and puffing about morality and honesty and about how I can be using a man accused of extreme unfaithfulness as an example in a section on Divine Connection. What you really want to know is what my stand is on the subject, admit it. So here it is.

I believe in being faithful in marriage (unless both parties agree otherwise). I believe I am neither God nor judge of what other people do. I believe nothing is absolute – we are all both good and bad, and trying to get better. I believe that what Tiger Woods did when he changed his swing is the most awesome act ever, and was definitely Divinely inspired, in a way that recent revelations may not have been – but who am I to judge? Who are you to judge?

All we can say is that there once was a man who dared do something that is inconceivable to most ... and on that pun, I will let the matter rest.

We are talking about integrating Power through Divine Connection through Appreciation. Appreciation is one of the most accessible doorways to connecting with the Divine. And we will look at cultivating both Appreciation and our Divine Connection in the final part of this section.

Cultivating Appreciation

Appreciation is more than gratitude.

Appreciation encompasses gratitude but extends beyond it. Appreciation is an all-embracing feeling of 'Life is great'! It's the acknowledgement that everything around us is as it should be – not as an idea or concept, but as a deep sense of well-being.

Appreciation is seeing what is before us daily: beautiful sunrises; awesome sunsets; the glory of rain; spectacular thunderstorms; soft, plump cheeks of babies; the lilting song of my daughter; a warm hug from my son; colourful wooden boats in the harbour; hazy mountains in the mist; knowing he will be home when I get there; the smell of freshly baked cookies; dew glistening on a morning petal; the sun stroking my naked back; mussel tang smell of the sea; the taste of butter on freshly cooked noodles; licking Nutella off a spoon; a sip of cappuccino; laughing with friends; a cloak of lush velvet; stroking the cat; milk-coated puppy breath; writing in my studio; singing; dancing, dancing, dancing! 'These are a few of the things I love ...'

Now list yours.
- Repeat daily in writing every morning for a month (preferably as a lifetime practice), and,
- Repeat every night to yourself (and to your beloved) just before you go to sleep
- Ask your children to tell you at dinner time what they appreciated in their day
- Write letters of appreciation to your friends, family, acquaintances, strangers who have impressed or moved you
- Literally count your blessings on a list
- Remind others of what they too can appreciate
- Tell others what you appreciate in them
- Appreciate!

Look at ways in which you can show appreciation for what you appreciate in your life. Spreading well-being is one of the gateways to wealth.

Cultivating Divine Connection

- What do you consider to be your connection with the Divine?

- How do you make the connection?
- Do you have a space and time in your life for Divine Connection?
- Do you listen to the still inner voice?
- Do you pay attention to dreams and premonitions?
- How do you communicate with the Divine?

Undertake to set aside time each day for Divine Connection. When you are connected to the Divine, you are aligned with your path. When you are aligned with your path, everything flows – including wealth!

Reflections of Gold

So far, we have looked at the 9 Levels of Wealth Consciousness, as progressive steps along our spiral path of holographic becomingness. Wow! Isn't that a fantastic sentence? What it means is that we have looked at our progress along the path of wealth creation as a series of developmental steps of increased consciousness, ability, and self along three triads. Beginning at Ignorance, Blame and Struggle; moving through Dependence, Co-dependence and Independence; to Comfort, Wealth and Affluence.

We have said that these levels are in constant motion, and that they are holographic – which means that at any level you may have to repeat other levels or go through all the levels several times – though each time you repeat a level, you will be doing so with greater awareness.

You have reflected on your own journey through the 9 Levels of Wealth Consciousness, using insightful questions, creative writing, and reflection. You have taken new decisions, committed to empowering action, and connected with feelings that will enhance and facilitate your Wealth Journey.

We have embraced this model as a map which will enable us to discover 'Where we are' so that we may rapidly move from there to 'Where we are going'. We have looked at where we are going as a state of beingness and reflected on that as a progressive, though interwoven scale of self-expression.

We looked at the 9 Dimensions of Self-expression as destinations of new beingness that we aspire to develop into on our Wealth Journey. We traced our development of self-expression from the first triad of Physicality, Identity and Sexuality, to Creativity, Spirituality and Authenticity arriving at Contentment, Service and Power. We have reflected on these aspects of ourselves and undertaken to be aware of and to cultivate qualities of self-expression that will enhance our Wealth Journey using creative processing.

The section that followed dealt with 'why you are not there' and introduced the 9 Wealth Challenges which, although they correlate with the various levels of Wealth Consciousness, can also present themselves anywhere along the Wealth Journey. In the 9 Wealth Challenges you had the opportunity to confront the challenge of opposites which appear along the journey to wealth and to integrate each challenge, allowing an empowering quality to emerge.

You have undergone an ENORMOUS amount of transformation – even if you just read the book without doing any of the processing (but do me a favour and please go back to the processing and do it – you will be so glad you did!). For those who have been regularly doing the processing, you know your life has changed. WELL DONE!

And as a reward for all your hard work, we will now look at 'How to get there' or 'The 11 Secrets of Wealth Creation'. Truly fabulous stuff! Don't you love it?

4

How To Get There

The 11 Secrets of Wealth Creation

1. Confront
2. Challenge
3. Believe
4. Dare
5. Trust
6. Empower
7. Know
8. Rejoice
9. Create
10. Deliver
11. Be(come)

In the 11 Secrets of Wealth Creation, you may notice that 'Believe' is not listed as the first secret, though in my work in general I go to great lengths to mention that without belief (in the impossible) nothing can be achieved. You will also find that though the first secret, 'Confront' expressed as the higher octave of Presence, does tie in with the Wealth Consciousness and Wealth Challenges models, the rest of the items do not necessarily do the same. Why is that?

I want to remind you (dear reader) that the world, life, events (and the very best of) models are not linear, not logical, do not necessarily follow an obvious line of thought. This is true of the wealth creation journey too. We are on a round planet, full of rounded ideas, theories, approaches, outlooks and ways to get from 'a' to 'b'. Or is it from 'a' to 'eight'?

The Wealth Journey is a spiral weaving in and then out of the centre, in ever expanding levels of being. So do not try to match everything up in your mind. Do not try to match the 9 Levels with the 9 Challenges, *and* the 9 Detours, 9 Dimensions, and 9 'I's' – for if you do, you will find the 11 Secrets a teensy bit of a problem ... Besides which, you will be on a mind journey instead of a journey of transformation.

While it's true that the 9 levels of Wealth Consciousness do correlate with the 9 Wealth Challenges – as I pointed out in those sections – the rest of the sections are not simply a rehash of that in different format. In other words, see each section in its entirety, for what it is, and work with what is given to you to work with.

These models represent different aspects within a multi-layered whole, within the focus of this book, which is a Wealth Journey.

So, let us begin:

The 11 Secrets of Wealth Creation

The 11 Secrets of Wealth Creation are qualities of beingness that we need to cultivate and integrate, which will enable us to successfully complete the Wealth Journey, as well as to move from one level of wealth becomingness to the next. Though we may have called upon some of these qualities and used them as tools to help us transform a wealth challenge in previous sections, here we are looking at the quality itself as a building block in the creation of a powerful wealth resonance (imagine a multifaceted pyramid) which will attract what we want to us.

When the quality of each wealth secret has been absorbed into your being, you will have arrived at your destination – you will have become your new wealthy self! As sure as God made little green apples! Don't you love it?

1. First Secret of Wealth Creation – Confront *(Developing Presence)*

Until you can stand up on your own two feet, firmly rooted to the ground, and call out to all who would listen (and even to those who would not):

> I AM! I AM HERE! I AM TAKING UP MY
> RIGHTFUL PLACE UPON THIS EARTH!

until you report to the start line with the willingness and readiness, and intent; not only to begin, but to complete the Wealth Journey – you cannot start, and you have not begun. To confront means to face, to look straight into: the eyes of every man (and woman); your fears and shadow; your aspirations and dreams; the obstacles you will face along the way; life in all its multifaceted hues of pain and joy; the fact that you could fail; the fact that you can (and WILL) succeed; the wealth you will create; what you will let go of along the way; what you will transform and embrace; the responsibilities you will encounter; the new wealthy self you are creating out of thin air.

So whereas we looked at Confront in terms of transcending Avoidance by unlocking the gift of Courage through Perseverance in the section on Wealth Challenges, here we look at Confront in a much more expansive context. We are looking at Confront as a quality of self or beingness we will cultivate, rather than as a necessary action in the process of transcending one of the Wealth Challenges. This is quite a significant distinction. Essentially, we are looking at the quality of Confront developing into the quality of Presence.

The ability to confront is definitely the first secret of wealth creation in terms of the Wealth Journey. It is one of the foundations of all success. Without it, nothing can be accomplished.

We used to play a little game, my business partner and I, of 'spot the successful person', while sitting in restaurants and coffee bars. You can try it too, if you like. You will notice people entering a casual restaurant or coffee bar fall into two categories – those who sheepishly hang around waiting to be told where to sit, even when empty tables abound; and those who boldly claim a table, sit down and order (yes, despite the 'wait to be seated' sign). Need I say more?

(And, yes, I am excluding the very 'formal' dining experience where you need to be formally seated. Though even here, you will notice a huge difference between those exuding an air of entitlement who approach allowing to be seated as a process of being served; and those who approach it as a process of being directed.)

Without the ability to confront, nothing can be accomplished

If you cannot claim a table for a cup of coffee, how on earth will you claim 27 million? Or even 1 million for that matter? If you cannot take ownership of your little spot of space which you carry around with you wherever you go, how will you take up the space of an empire? We are talking about Confront becoming so imprinted in your energy field that it radiates as Presence.

So, first and foremost, before you can even start your Wealth Journey you need to understand, develop, and cultivate taking up your place in the world – or the ability to confront. You need to be so comfortable in your own shoes that you can lay claim to a space bigger than yourself – in other words, a coffee table; a whole restaurant; a business; and then an empire.

Your awareness of this fact is the start. Begin by examining how you take up space in the world. Examine your level of Presence. And remember, if you can ace the little things, the big things will take care of themselves. So let's start with the little things:

Over the next few days, observe yourself as you go through your life. Take a notepad with you and reflect lightly and compassionately on what you see, without judgement. Ask yourself the following questions, as you observe. Later, write for two minutes on each prompt. Let your hand write. Allow what emerges to emerge without censoring.

Reflecting on my Ability to Confront

- How do I take up my space in the world?
- How do I allow others to interact with my space?
- In what situations am I thrown off balance?

- Where/how do I shrink?
- What do I believe in the moment I allow myself to shrink?
- What do I feel in the moment I shrink?
- What can I do to ensure I hold my space?
- What do I need to believe in order to hold my space?

How does it feel to take up my space in the world?

Take any decisions you need to take as a result of this knowledge. Formulate a plan of action and do it. **Connect with the feel-good feeling!** *Make any changes you need to make in your life. Keep it simple. Keep it light. Keep it fun.*

Developing Presence – Claiming your space in the world

You may remember we began the process of cultivating your ability to confront in the section on wealth challenges, by introducing you to a number of light activities, such as saying no, doing what you wouldn't normally do and so on. Now in order to embrace this quality fully, you need to cultivate it as a practice. You need to diligently, carefully and regularly stand your ground. Not because you are trying to be difficult, not because you have to, but because it is the first leg, and one of the cornerstones, of what you need in order to succeed.

When the world is against the idea that will make you a billionaire, or if the best coaches don't believe your approach will make you the best golfer the world has ever known (like Tiger Woods), or when everyone wants you to give up, and all 'evidence' in the 'real world' points to giving up being a good idea, then *you will need the ability to stand your ground*.

When the first bank says 'no' to funding the project that will make you a billionaire, and then the second and the twentieth say no too, or the first nineteen publishers reject your best-seller (as they did mine – of course it will become a best-seller!), are you going to crumble and fall apart? Or will you confront each 'no' as if it were just another small step towards bringing you closer to your goal? To do that, to carry on, undeterred, *you need the ability to Confront.*

So you need to practise this skill – for it *is* a skill. You need to diligently, carefully, and regularly stand your ground. You need to stand firmly, without crumbling. You need to be able to face whatever reality throws your way – effortlessly, gracefully, with dignity and with Presence. And then continue undeterred. That's the trick.

Let me give you a small example of what happened to me the other day. I was in a large shopping centre. A few minutes before closing time I rushed towards the doors of a large, well-known store, but I was not in time – the security guard shut the door firmly (just as I got there) and locked it, while grimly shaking his head. I beckoned to him to open. I tried to gesture that I wanted a word with him. I wanted to walk through the store, to another exit (visible from the one we were at), where my car was parked. I did not want to shop. This I explained to him very nicely and politely and with great friendliness.

Whereas walking across to the other exit of this store would take only a few moments, getting there by walking all the way around half the shopping centre and a considerable part of the parking lot, would take an enormous amount of time. I was tired, and besides, I did not see the point.

The security guard said 'no'. He turned his back. A saga ensued during which he was not only rude and obnoxious, but he refused to call the manager when I requested this. Time passed. I was joined by other women in a similar plight. For a long time he ignored us, continued to be rude in response to our entreaties each time he opened the door to let a shopper out. Now this security guard was going way beyond the call of duty. He was not merely trying to do his job. He was abusing his position to be plain and simple nasty.

I was beginning to consider that walking the long way round to my car would have taken less time after all ... But I was not prepared to stand down. So we stood, and we waited, until the manager eventually came.

I exchanged a few words with the manager and we were allowed through. I did not cause a scene. I merely thanked the manager and went to my car. I let the other women address the security guard's rudeness.

Why did I do it? Because I couldn't do otherwise. Was it worth it? Oh yes! I felt good! It reinforced my sense of winning, and of justice, and of being able to cause things to happen in the world. All of which we need to practise – *all the time*. If I had stood down, if I had simply hung my head and taken the long way round, I would have left feeling deflated, tired, maybe angry, with a sense of injustice. More importantly, if I had not stood my ground, would I still be here writing this book, or would I have given up writing when my first book was initially rejected? That is the Real question.

One last thing: Don't think that Confront and Presence has to be a bolshy, arrogant, aggressive sort of attitude, that as a gentle, peace-loving soul you may automatically want to shrink from. Some of the nicest, kindest, and sweetest people in the world have enormous Confront and Presence – witness Mother Teresa, the Dalai Lama, and my husband Shaun.

Shaun is a gentle, gentle soul. In typical Piscean fashion he always sees the best in others, empathising, understanding, charming his way through most situations in a soft voice. But behold how he stands his ground so very firmly when crossed on a matter of importance, or when gross inefficiency rears its head to a point that even he cannot ignore. Observe the effect of his British understatement, 'No, this will not do. This is not acceptable. I am going to put the phone down now otherwise I may say something rude.' Truly, I heard him say these very words! (I was in hysterics of course! But then I'm Greek, and would have probably been rude first, and put the phone down later ...). Yes, Shaun is one of my great teachers.

The point is you can stand your ground, cultivate Presence, and create results, without losing the essence of who you are. After all, what we are doing is cultivating and sharpening and refining your own unique 'you-ness'. Because, in the words of Dr Seuss,

'There is no one more you-er than you'!

Developing Presence – Performing Successful Actions

- Look for opportunities to stand your ground – don't compromise
- List ways in which you can cultivate Presence (e.g. giving your opinion to a group) – do it
- Develop your ability to Confront as part of your daily practice
- Don't take no for an answer (exercise good sense on this one – don't coerce)
- Allow no one to change the way you act or feel
- Connect with the feel good feeling of winning, as often as you can, daily
- Make a stand for justice – whatever that means for you

A final suggestion: Observe the way you dress. Even when Presence radiates from your very being, it may be hard for most people to take you seriously if you face them in your tatty garden clothes. It may be clichéd (and it is), but Presence can be greatly enhanced with the right wardrobe and look. Never mind if you think 'it shouldn't matter what you wear' – it does. I don't want to wear business suits or high-heeled shoes any more – but, let's be honest now, if you saw my picture on the back cover of this book in some cheap tatty tracksuit, looking all straggly and unkempt, would you have bought the book? I didn't think so.

2. Second Secret of Wealth Creation – Challenge *(Cultivating Awakening)*

The second secret of wealth creation is Challenge. Challenge here means Awakening. To challenge means to question, to look beyond the norm and the obvious, to be open to other possibilities. And, again, remember that the various secrets of wealth creation are not linear. It is not a matter of first you cultivate this quality and then you cultivate the next one. This is the case only up to a point. In reality all these qualities exist simultaneously, in a circular, 'layers of an onion' sort of way, as we have discussed before.

The quality of Challenge or Awakening is probably one of the impulses that initiates your wealth quest. Without it, you cannot continue. You begin the Wealth Journey because you are questioning the status quo in one or another way. Certainly you are challenging your current situation. You may be saying things like, 'Wait a minute, why can't I too be wealthy?' or 'Hang on, I think I can do that better than it's been done before.'

The quality of Challenge is deeply ingrained in all successful people. It is the ability to question the way things are and to offer new solutions. It's the willingness to do something in a way that has never been done before – to rise to the challenge, so to speak. Challenge is also an extension of Presence or Confront because it's the ability to face *and overcome*, well ... challenges.

In my previous example about being shut out of the store, all the women were confronting the situation, but I was challenging it. I was finding the solution – refusing to leave, speaking to the security guard over and over again, calling for the manager, speaking on behalf of the group. I made it possible for the other women to stay and confront. (What a hero!)

Yes, challenge is heroic stuff. It's the awakening of action. But before that, challenge is an attitude of mind. One of the greatest challenges I sometimes face is when I deal with people in a company who want me to show them how to make quantum leaps in productivity and profit margins, but are not prepared to consider even looking at doing anything they have been doing in a different way.

'No, no,' they say, 'you don't understand, this is a very specific industry. It only works if we do things in this very specific way that we've always been doing it.' This attitude always boggles my mind.

All great fortunes, innovations, quantum leaps, and expansions were made possible because one day someone *changed something!* Think of that! Really, really, think about it, and reflect on your own life from this perspective.

It may seem very obvious, and it is, but

While things remain the same, nothing can change!

Let's try that again – *while things remain the same, nothing can change!* Really embrace this truism. Consider that for anything to be different, *something has to change!* To do that, you need to take up the challenge. You need to challenge, which in this context also means to question.

Let us look at questioning for a moment. Quite central to my approach, as you have probably gathered by now (even if you have not read all of my books, or attended any of my courses), is the use of skilful questioning. In fact much of my processing involves creating a shift through the proper use of questions. I believe that once you have found the right question, the answer will automatically be revealed. I will go as far as to say that contained in the kernel of a skilful question is a skilful answer.

Learning to ask useful questions is a skill we can develop. Often, when we face challenges we ask 'Why?' Is it useful to ask 'Why'? Can it help us? Is it empowering? Can it assist us to move forward? These are the sorts of questions we should be asking of our questions.

'Why?' is a very disempowering approach to problem solving. It does not help us. It is not useful. It only serves to lay blame or to diminish our power. It is a childish question. 'Why?' keeps us stuck on that question, as our mind tries to work with and negotiate the question itself, instead of being directed towards the answer.

We need to ask 'How ...?' to get what we want; to get the answer; to find missing pieces of the puzzle; to become. We need to ask 'Where ...? the answers many be hidden; to look; to go next. We need to ask 'When ...?' may be the best time to do something; move forward; execute our plan. We need to ask 'Which ...?'option is better; 'What ...?' should I be focusing on, or doing to achieve my goals.

When we ask the right questions, the answers are revealed

Reflecting on my ability to Challenge

- What are the important questions in my life at this time?
- Which areas of my life need new questions?
- Which questions have I been neglecting to ask? About my Wealth Journey? About life?
- What help do I need?
- What can I improve, or do better?
- What do I need to challenge?

How does it feel to stand grounded in my own space as I shake the world around me?

*Take any decisions you need to take as a result of this knowledge. Formulate a plan of action and do it. **Connect with the feel-good feeling!** Make any changes you need to make in your life. Keep it simple. Keep it light. Keep it fun.*

Cultivating Challenge – Standing up for what you believe

Challenge is the awakening of action. It is also the awakening of self. It is the active element of Confront. It is taking up your position in space. It is standing up for what you believe, and even going as far as defending it. It is that point in the creation cycle when you have taken the decision to go forward with your intent.

Contained in the kernel of a skilful question
is a skilful answer

As you will recall, you are tested at many different points along your Wealth Journey. Throughout the Wealth Journey you may be called upon to Challenge. Sometimes the challenge is about breaking into a new level of being, sometimes it's standing up for your truth in the midst of temptation, at other times it's literally braving the forces (either energetic or literal) that may be trying to oppose you or distract you, or bring you down. These 'forces' are often internal. Perhaps it's your mind that is challenging you by casting doubt, or throwing some old beliefs at you. Perhaps it's the media spreading fear of success.

Either way you need to cultivate the ability to stand your ground and defend your position. Defending your position sometimes involves defending your wealth, your new idea, your new product, the fact that you believe you will succeed. It means remaining connected with the still inner core while the world around you is shaken up or doubting.

Defending your position begins at the core of your being. It is an act of connecting with your centre, knowing what you will and will not allow into your world. It is the foundation of belief. Awakening is also the development of self-knowledge. You need to know what you stand for, and then you need to be prepared to stand up for that.

In the *Money Well*™ you are invited to look at your parameters – which lines you will cross and which you will not. This is very important on our Wealth Journey. Knowing what you will challenge and what you will not, knowing what is important to you – in other words, your value system – lies at the foundation of success.

So Challenge relates to placing our feet firmly on the ground, grinding them into the ground itself, then, as my Chinese t'ai-chi teacher used to say as we stood in horse position – 'legs strong in the ground, long root like tree trunk, solid, cannot move; but arms light, like leaves, moving in wind'.

Mastering the secret of Challenge is crucial if you are to succeed on your Wealth Journey. It begins with questioning the status quo and culminates in a desire and commitment to create change.

We cultivate Challenge through regularly practising Standing Up – for our beliefs, our decisions, our commitments, our dreams, our values, our principles. We say 'No'. We say 'I can'.

We say 'I will'
We do what it takes

Cultivating Challenge – Performing Successful Actions

- Look for 3 new ways to approach current challenges in life and wealth. Execute.
- Consider 8 situations, people, beliefs, attitudes you need to challenge
- Create new solutions for these challenges. Execute your decisions
- List your 5 most important values in life
- Decide to uphold these values and make any adjustments in your life to accommodate this decision
- Connect with the feel-good feeling of winning, as often as you can daily

When you are ready not only to stand up for and defend what you believe in, but are also willing to go one step further and question the status quo, consider new possibilities, and open yourself to new ways of looking at the world; the world of new possibilities and miracles and wonders will open up for you too.

Because, let's face it, if you want amazing things to happen, you need to be open to things that you now cannot begin to imagine – be open to that!

3. Third Secret of Wealth Creation – Believe *(The Opening of the Heart)*

Before anyone can believe you can do it, *you* must believe you can do it. Before anyone will believe it can happen, *you* must believe it can happen. Before anything can change, *you* must believe it can change. Before your dream can manifest, *you* must create it, believe in it, nurture it, and coax it into being.

If *you* don't believe it, who can? If you are not willing to swear by it, who will? If you are not positively-convinced-without-a-shadow-of-a-doubt that it will happen, why should anyone else be? Remember in the film *Finding Neverland* how the fairies and magical kingdoms began to fade as people stopped believing in them? Well, that's exactly it! When you create a dream, when you want to turn some 'hare-brained notion' into a living, breathing (and dare I say highly profitable) reality, then you Absolutely *Have* to Believe, as the first order of business.

And, yes, I say 'hare-brained' because if we really analyse some of the success stories, well ... Who would believe the idea of bacon-flavoured everything (from mayonnaise to lip gloss) which, I saw on Oprah the other day, some entrepreneurs had made a fortune out of? How about fluffy toys that you build, complete with their own wardrobes of clothing, right down to the underwear? And what about a story about a boy wizard that adults can read? Or themed hotels complete with make-believe jungles and man-made beaches with waves? What about reality programmes? The list is quite endless, if you think about it.

Before anyone else can believe it, you must believe it

So having the deep grounding and preparation of Confront and Challenge under your belt – and you will need both in large doses to support your Belief – you are ready to create on the non-physical. This is where all dreams begin, with an idea. And that idea has to be fed with your faith and unwavering trust if it has any hope of becoming born into action.

I have heard so many people say things like – 'Well I'm writing this book, but I'm not sure anyone will want to buy it … you know how hard it is to get into a publishing house … and anyway no one makes money out of writing … so … I don't know …' Can you possibly imagine this person succeeding in their venture?

Or they say, 'Well, I have this idea for a business, but "everyone" knows that times are hard … and you need money to make money … and besides, "according to statistics" (*I especially hate that one!*) most businesses fail in the first year … so I don't know … besides I have a good job, which is quite rare these days, so I'd better hold onto it … anyway it's not like I want lots of money … I just want to be comfortable …' Yes, I would definitely suggest that anyone who speaks that way about their dream, anyone who is so dismissive of their proposed creation and so obviously does not believe, should stick to their day job! And that's more good advice.

Believing is one of the cornerstones of the wealth creation

process. Without belief nothing will happen! In *Money Alchemy*™ you are given the opportunity to uncover and process your beliefs around wealth. The *Money Well*™ also contains some very powerful energetic transformations, enabling you to change the beliefs that don't serve you into ones that do.

Let's look at Belief, and how we can cultivate it.

Reflecting on my ability to Believe

- What do I believe about wealth/the wealthy/success/my ability to achieve what I want?
- What do I not believe?
- What would I like to believe?
- Which beliefs do I need to nurture?
- Which beliefs do I need to let go of?
- What are the beliefs on which I base my life?

How does it feel to believe anything is possible?

Take any decisions you need to take as a result of this knowledge. Formulate a plan of action and do it. **Connect with the feel-good feeling!** *Make any changes you need to make in your life. Keep it simple. Keep it light. Keep it fun.*

Cultivating Belief – Opening the Heart

You absolutely need to believe! Instead of doubting, you need to convince yourself, and your mind, and your emotions, and every fibre of your being that what you hope to create is not only possible, but that you will cause it to come into being. Instead of negative scenarios, you need to think of all the reasons why it can work. Instead of listening to nay-sayers, you need to list all the arguments in favour of the success of your venture. Instead of thinking how it could fail, you need to constantly remind yourself why your vision is going to be the best thing that happened in the world since sliced bread. Instead of anxiety and fear, you need to connect with the fun and excitement and enthusiasm of seeing your dream complete. Instead of planning what you will do if it doesn't work, you need to spend much time considering how to contain and accommodate the *realisation* of your dream.

And you need to be doing all of that, *in the face of a total lack of evidence or tangible proof of any kind* that what you are trying to create is in fact in any way possible or even plausible. That is believing! But the good news is that you only need belief the size of a mustard seed to move a whole mountain – so really, it's not as hard as it seems, if all you're trying to do is get a book on the shelves, is it?

The tricky part is that to enter into that trusting space you have to pass a camel through the eye of a needle, or become like a child again, which requires that you open your heart. Opening the heart means many things. Firstly, we need to listen to our heart so we may know our 'heart's desire'. Then we need to be ready and willing to enter into manifesting that desire through believing that this is in fact what is best for us, and perhaps not what our mother or father or fortune-teller told us. That's an act of claiming our power.

Belief has nothing to do with what's out there, or what's not
out there
Belief is a space, a resonance, a state of being

But the minute we do that, we are also taking responsibility. We cannot lay the blame elsewhere any more. (*Drat! Don't you hate when that happens ...?)* Finally, and perhaps the part that is hardest, when we commit to bringing into being what we truly want, we make ourselves vulnerable. We are in one sense 'wearing our heart on our sleeve'. There is so much more at stake emotionally. We don't want to face becoming disappointed, or to fail in the thing we *truly* want.

Yet believing in our hearts, in our dreams, and in ourselves, is the simplest and easiest and most effortless of things to do. It's the resistance that's hard. Belief, like anything else can be cultivated and practised. Belief has nothing to do with what's out there, or what's not out there. Belief has nothing to do with proof or what is visible. Belief is a space, a resonance, a state of being that is childlike and open and trusting. And it's easy because it's actually our natural state of mind.

Cultivating Belief – Doing Three Impossible Things before breakfast

- Decide to believe in 3 unlikely things, and watch them happen. (You can!)
- Decide to believe in 3 improbable things, and watch them happen. (You can!)
- Decide to believe in 3 impossible things, and bring them into being. (You can!)
- Create 3 new wealth enhancing beliefs and use them in your daily speech
- Create a list of 9 reasons why your dream will work
- Write a list of 9 reasons why you will always succeed, no matter what you do
- Write a list of 9 reasons why you believe in yourself
- Connect with the innocent, joyful, playful, anticipatory feeling of 'anything is possible, and it's about to happen!'
- Believe all of the above

The good news is that when we commit 'heart and soul' to the path that makes our heart sing, to creating what we truly want, we usually find that it is something for which we have a natural aptitude. It's something we enjoy and love doing, something that comes more easily to us than other things, something that may even seem so effortless that we struggle to classify it as 'work'. We may not even recognise it as a talent or gift. If we commit to pursuing a path that is closely aligned with our ground plan then succeeding in that thing should and will be a lot easier than struggling along a path that we do not resonate with. That makes sense, doesn't it? And it's true. And it starts with believing!

What you need to believe in the most is yourself

4. Fourth Secret of Wealth Creation – Dare *(Inspired Action)*

Daring is one of the least venerated or discussed or written about secrets of wealth creation. Goals, having a dream, persistence and perseverance, faith and trust and maybe even gratitude are the better known ingredients for the money making cauldron, but Daring, that most precious of qualities, is often completely overlooked.

What would you attempt to do, if you knew you could not fail?

Daring is about challenging parameters, stretching them, bending them, making pretzels out of them so that they can accommodate your dream. There's a very fine line between that and contravening parameters altogether – which some people get carried away and do – thus giving the whole wealth creation process a bad name!

Daring is called *thrassos* in Greek – it's very much a masculine quality, though one should not become remiss enough to forget all the great women possessed of this quality. Witness the Amazonian women for example, removing their left breast for the betterment of their sport – perhaps that's zeal, or sports fanaticism … None the less, it's also *thrassos*.

Daring is about 'no fear', it's a tongue-in-cheek audaciousness. Daring is cheeky and inventive. It's dreaming up truly outlandish and creative ways around obstacles. Daring is a bold, chest-out, oh-what-the-heck-we're-gonna-get-wet-but-it's-worth-it attitude. Daring is ingenious and courageous. It contains and transcends both Confront and Challenge, and it most definitely arises out of total and absolute Belief.

Daring is the commitment to make it happen – any which way. (Now I did warn about totally ignoring rules and parameters earlier, so I will not keep repeating this: going illegal is **not** what I am inferring here – end of this chat.) Daring is deciding you will make it happen – no matter what it takes. And usually what it takes is a radical shift in thinking in the first instance.

What this means is going beyond limitation, expanding the ceiling, reconfiguring beliefs in what is and what is not possible. Daring is sticking your neck out, putting yourself on the line, going out of your comfort zone, and all of this first starts inside your head. You have to master and integrate Belief first. You cannot break new boundaries if you do not believe – because quite simply you will not believe you can do it.

Children have oodles of daring – they keep pushing parameters. And it's our challenge as parents to keep safe boundaries going on the one hand while not crushing their will and daring on the other.

Daring is the commitment to make it happen – no matter what

A little note on debt here: The Daring I am talking about is not getting an overdraft, or continuously increasing it, or juggling around your credit facilities and bond. Yes, once in a while it takes daring to try and raise a large sum of money, but raising debt as an ongoing pattern is not the daring I am hoping you will cultivate.

First you have to dare to believe it. Often this is the Daring that is challenged first. People may ask how you dare to imagine that you will succeed where others have failed. They will want to know how you dare to be so optimistic in the face of so much failure all around you, and what qualifies you for such Daring, and most of all, 'How dare you imagine you can transcend?'

It is very important to let as few people as possible in on your anticipated dreams and plans. Certainly in the creation and planning stages, and in the early doing stages, keep your own counsel. Keep the new little seed in the dark ground, in the womb, while it grows. Protect the seedling, and keep it out of the harmful rays of nay-sayers and non-believers.

Let's look at Daring, and how we can cultivate it.

Reflecting on my ability to Dare

- What do I believe about daring?
- What do I believe about my daring?
- What do I believe I would dare to do?

- What do I believe I would not dare to do?
- What would I like to be able to dare to do?
- What would I need to believe to be able to dare anything I wanted to?
- What can I dare do today?

How does it feel to dare to do what I really want?

Take any decisions you need to take as a result of this knowledge. Formulate a plan of action and do it. **Connect with the feel-good feeling!** *Make any changes you need to make in your life. Keep it simple. Keep it light. Keep it fun.*

Cultivating Daring – The Beginning of Action

The secret of Daring is seizing the moment – taking the leap. In the heart-seed of daring is mischief and fun – in other words, play, and that often arises on the spur of the moment, and invariably involves asking 'Why not?'

Once, I had a very important dentist appointment set many months before, which my boss at the time waved away as less important than some spur-of-the-moment motivational type meeting, making it quite clear that non-attendance was not an option. He was also not open to discussion on the matter. I sent a tape recorder to that meeting with a note and went to the dentist. There was much laughter, and my move was talked about for many months, but I did not otherwise pick up any problem at work.

Many times, while I was an investment consultant, I followed my instinct on the spur of the moment. I 'popped in', unannounced and without appointment, to see people usually too busy to be seen even by appointment. Two were doctors, as I recall. These were people who on many previous occasions had refused to have their portfolios managed, even though they were losing money and needed our services badly.

So in I would sweep when the mood or the *thrassos* took over. 'I just need a minute,' I would tell the secretary, and dash for the prospective client's door. Once in, I would confront the startled prospect with something quite zippy like 'Right, I have come to sign you up for management today. I think it's time.' (Hold the space ...) Upon which the person would laugh, and invariably reply 'Oh, okay.' Unbelievable? Believe it!

In a tree, Daring is the branches and leaves. Confront, Challenge and Belief are the trunk that supports and underpins Daring. Daring is not serious, not uptight, it can roll with the punches, laugh off temporary defeat if it comes, move nimbly out of harm's way. Daring bends and yields and finds new ways around the wind. Daring is inventive.

The wind never bothers Daring, because Daring does not try to oppose it, it moves with it. The leaves and seed pods take advantage of the wind to spread their seeds and grow. Seed pods are poised, ready, sometimes they wait for a whole season for the slightest breath of wind to take them to their destination.

We too must be ready for that moment, that one moment that we need to seize with both hands when it comes. That is also daring. Sometimes we need not so much to initiate action as to respond. Someone opens a door, or offers to open a door. Do we grab the moment and say 'Yes!'? Or do we start to consider all the reasons we shouldn't go through the door? Or couldn't? Or look for the problems, or doubt the door is there or that it is open at all?

*We must be ready for that moment, that one moment
that we need to seize with both hands when it comes,
that moment when the door is opened*

Some examples: A successful business friend offered to help an acquaintance who was struggling in a related business – she said, 'I can help you, whatever help you need, let me know.' She was making the offer because she is a really good and kind human being, and because she could, and because it was not a big deal for her to offer the help, though it would have been a huge deal for the other person, who unfortunately just never took up the offer.

Once, a few years ago, I offered to help out a business that was closing its doors, as I had an interest in investing in that field. I wrote, 'Let me know how I can help, I have lots of business background and experience. (And incidentally lots of cash – which I did not mention.)' To this day I have never received a reply to that email.

There is a book available called *Pronoia Is the Antidote for Paranoia* (Rob Brezny), which suggests that the world is constantly offering us opportunity to flourish and prosper, that doors are constantly opening, people all around us are trying to help, everyone and everything around us is conspiring to help us succeed! If only we would notice. *Believe that!*

But ... we need to open our arms. We need to believe that. We need to take the help. Accept the help. Dare to imagine that it is there and for goodness sake, just open the door when opportunity knocks, or, when the door is opened for you, have the good sense to simply walk through!

So the question (and it's a good one) boils down to this:

Do you dare to imagine that in some mysterious and
inexplicable way
an absolutely magical and profound and totally effortless path
exists for you to receive all that your heart desires?

Please pay special attention to the words 'effortless' and
'receive'. And when the answer to that question is 'yes', then
the question is:

Do you dare to take it?

Sometimes all you need do is put out your hand. Will you
dare do that?

Cultivating Daring – Taking the First Step

- Decide to dare to do 3 things you would love to be able to
  dare to do. Do them
- Look out for dropped coins along your path. Pick them
  up with gratitude
- Look for open doors (metaphorical). Go through them
- Open yourself up to seeing spontaneous beneficial
  moments. Seize them
- Take help offered to you. Be open to help from others
- Ask for help. Receive it with gratitude
- Give help where you can, without thought of reward or
  praise

Put your intent on always seeing the many opportunities
and gifts that are around, and make a firm commitment to
receiving them and asking for more. That's Daring, and it's
very closely linked to the next secret – Trust.

5. Fifth Secret of Wealth Creation – Trust *(Arousing Authority)*

You probably think trust and authority are on opposite poles, yet trust is nothing more than internal authority. When you have trust, what you have is inner conviction. When you rely on trust, you are relying on your inner compass, knowing, conviction, intuition – sometimes over and above your five senses or your logical mind.

Trust is not some namby-pamby, wussy, airy-fairy, new-agey predisposition for the fanatically religious or for the feeble-minded. Trust is not unscientific, or old-fashioned, or no longer suitable for this dark and dangerous age. Trust is not a trap set to lure us into the hands of evil. Yet many of us think this way.

> When you have trust, what you have is inner conviction

Trust is something that many have become highly suspicious of. And the more technologically advanced we become (which was supposed to result in much more leisure time), the more possessions we acquire (which was supposed to offer us more ease), the more affluent we become (which was supposed to make us much happier), the less we trust our world and those around us. Now that's a fact for most people.

When we cultivate trust we are cultivating the part of ourselves that knows. We are also opening ourselves up to the beneficial forces all around us – the universe, or God, or Angels, or the Divine, or Universal Mind – depending on our belief. When we can trust, it means we can believe in ourselves. When we can believe in ourselves it means we trust our decisions, our views, and our direction. We can then trust our intuition and our inner guidance. Then we can believe that what we set out to do will, in fact, be done. We can believe in our projects and our dreams. We can believe that it will happen. Why? Because we trust ourselves – simple.

When we fully trust ourselves we become connected with our own authority, and we speak and act with power. We can then say, 'Yes, I will write a best-seller'. How do I know it will be so? Because I said so, and I trust myself. We can say, 'Yes, I will start a profitable gardening business and it will flourish and prosper'. How do I know it will be so? Because I said so, and I believe so, and I trust myself. Therefore it will be so. That is trust.

Do you trust yourself? Do you believe yourself? Do you trust yourself to do what you set out to do? You are the most important person in the world to trust.

Trust enables and allows your inner voice of authority to emerge. Once that happens, you do not need anyone to tell you if you will succeed or to give you statistics or even to create a business proposal because once you are fully connected with trust – you simply know.

Think for a moment about any of the well-known, highly successful people in the world and consider whether total belief in their inner knowing – in other words, trust – is an integral component of their being and, ultimately, of their creations. Sol Kerzner creates a 'Lost City'. Donald Trump creates Trump Towers. Richard Branson plans trips to the moon. Mother Teresa, a penniless nun, sets off to India by train to feed and clothe millions of homeless people. They trust their vision and so others can trust it also. They do not quaver and shake and question. They do not say 'I wonder if it will work?' or 'Maybe I should check the statistics first'. They trust and they go for it. That's authority.

Let's look at trust, and how we can cultivate it.

Trust allows your inner voice of authority to emerge

Reflecting on my ability to Trust

- What do I trust?
- What do I not trust?
- What do I need to believe to totally trust?
- Where is my authority?
- Who is in charge of my trust?
- What do I need to do to regain trust in myself?

How does it feel to trust that all will be well?

Take any decisions you need to take as a result of this knowledge. Formulate a plan of action and do it. **Connect with the feel-good feeling!** *Make any changes you need to make in your life. Keep it simple. Keep it light. Keep it fun.*

Cultivating Trust – Arousing Authority

Many people joke, 'I trust myself, it's others I have a problem with.' This is not a helpful approach. While we do not trust, we cannot grow. Of course the old proverb 'Trust in God but tie your camel first' must prevail; then, we need to trust. Or rather we need to start with trust, then tie our camel, then continue to trust.

Successful people become successful because they trust their ideas, their intuition and their plans. They trust others to run their expanding businesses, to be in charge, to make decisions on their behalf, to handle their money, to spend their money, to grow their money. They trust themselves to pick the right products and people and operating basis, they trust their timing to buy and sell assets. Yes, sometimes they get it wrong. Yes, they do get business plans and other input, but first order of business – they trust.

To trust you need to transcend fear. This does not necessarily mean you feel no fear – it simply means you do it anyway, believing and trusting in the best possible outcome – the outcome you believe will come to pass. Trust is a very necessary component in Daring as well as in Challenge and Confront.

Trust starts with you. Can you trust yourself? Implicitly? Can you say yes, I am totally and completely trustworthy – anywhere, any time, I can be relied upon? For if you want to trust others, and if you want to trust the universe to deliver, then you need to trust yourself first.

You need to believe in yourself and in your word and in your ability to call things and bring them into being. The more true you are to your word, the more power your word will contain. The more power your word contains, the more authority your word will represent, and the more others will be drawn to deliver on your vision.

To trust you need to open yourself to every possibility – to possible failure, to possible success, to possible ridicule, to expansion and growth and to change. We do not always know how that change will unfold, and so we often refuse to trust simply because we do not want to risk change.

We also don't want to risk disappointment. The difference between successful people and others is that successful people are not afraid to get it wrong, to 'fail', to have a setback. Adversity does not dissolve their trust. It does not cause them to pause and stumble or question their original decision. It does not bring their trust into question.

The problem is that when we hear the success stories of others, we focus on the beginning and the end. The middle, and how long that took, and how many temporary setbacks were involved is somehow lost in the telling. I have noticed for example that many highly acclaimed writers only become so after their tenth or twelfth book – this gives me hope. Yet when we are first presented with their success story, it seems as if the person wrote a book and it became a best-seller and now they are on the Oprah list, and it all happened in the space of a year or a few short months. No, actually, in most cases (though of course there are exceptions) that writer wrote many books, over many years, before the success emerged.

In fact, on this very point, Malcolm Gladwell in his book *Outliers* states that even what we consider to be 'genius' – the likes of Mozart for example or Bill Gates or the Beatles – is the result of a huge amount of hard work – 10 000 hours is what Gladwell sets it at – before the 'tipping point' (and he has a book on that too ...)

But we are talking here of trust. And we are saying that throughout all that time, and possible adversity, through all those 10 000 hours, we need to continue to trust. And we need to stick our neck out enough to become our first line of authority on our Wealth Journey.

Cultivating Trust – Developing Authority

- Set aside 10 minutes daily to sit quietly and listen to the small inner voice
- Increase to 20 minutes daily after two weeks. Keep your eyes open, glancing down with eyes unfocused on a spot in front of you
- Look daily for input in the form of signs and wonders – listen to and feel the message

- Record your dreams daily – ask yourself what they mean
- Take the decision to always believe your 'gut feeling'
- Ask your image of the Divine for guidance. Listen. Follow. Trust
- Decide to trust yourself from this moment on
- Decide that you will attract others into your life who you can trust as much as you trust yourself

Our quiet inner voice is always there to guide us. We need to make the time and space to listen. We need to trust this voice beyond everything else. We need to put this voice and viewpoint above all the facts and figures and advice. We need to learn to believe that the Divine spark within us is also the Divine spark within others and we need to trust that too.

6. Sixth Secret of Wealth Creation – Empower *(Sowing Kindness)*

When trust has taken root in your heart and mind, it begins to manifest as action – the action of empowerment. Empowerment is a critical step in wealth creation, and here we focus on the empowerment of others, for without the help of others, no empire has ever been created.

You cannot single-handedly be all over the globe, all at once, running a huge corporation. To flourish and prosper, to *really* flourish and prosper, you need to help others flourish and prosper too.

This takes many shapes and forms, and begins with kindness to self, and acknowledgement of self. For unless you can contain, nurture, and empower yourself first; you will be unable to either see or to cultivate this attitude in respect of others.

Many extremely wealthy people (I think here of Felix Denis, a British entrepreneur) believe that one of the greatest secrets of success is finding and employing others with better abilities and skills and talents than one's own. This is quite an enlightened viewpoint. It is the viewpoint of someone who is so self-empowered that he does not think that others with more ability, talent, or skill are a threat. This is the attitude of a winner, and indeed evidence points to the fact.

However, until we radiate and are deeply rooted in our own sense of empowerment we will not easily be able to grant others the right to be as wonderful and powerful (if not more so) as ourselves. We are generally raised to think of winning and losing. And there is always one winner. Sure, there's talk of win-win but mostly this is pc lip service. Mostly, when we say win-win, what we are really saying is that we do not want the other person to be in a more powerful position than ourselves. We generally do not imply that we are willing or able to take turns at winning, or to have someone else be better at something than ourselves – particularly if we are employing them.

Recently I was approached via email by someone with a wealth-related newsletter who offered to circulate my details to their database if I would do the same for them. When I agreed, I was asked for the size of my database, because, and I quote 'this must be a win-win situation'.

Becoming self-empowered means you are able to take credit. Think about those words for a while. And *before you can take credit, you must give credit* – that is the correct sequence in the natural order of give and take. So you start by giving yourself credit. Then, you can give credit to others, and soon credit will come back to you. Is language not a very wonderful thing?

Let's look at empowerment of self and others.

Reflecting on Empowerment of Self and Others

- What do I take credit for?
- What do I not take credit for?
- Who decides that I am winning?
- How do I empower others? At home? At work?
- How can I give myself more credit?
- How can I empower others?

How does it feel to be empowered?

Take any decisions you need to take as a result of this knowledge. Formulate a plan of action and do it. **Connect with the feel-good feeling!** *Make any changes you need to make in your life. Keep it simple. Keep it light. Keep it fun.*

Becoming self-empowered means you are able to take credit; you start by giving yourself credit, you become an asset

Cultivating Kindness – Developing Empowerment

We do not usually think of money and kindness in the same breath. Yet, if we pause for a moment, we recognise the incredible amount of kindness which is generated and spread as a result of money. Kindness and compassion are entering the workplace more and more, to replace the old paradigms.

First we need to be kind to ourselves. We need to become our own inner parents – offering guidance, support, encouragement, saying 'well done'! Then we need to recognise that the divine spark (whatever our understanding of that is) resides in the heart of all. All people want to be happy. Then we need to develop the desire to help others, recognising that as we help them, we help and empower ourselves.

When we help others achieve their goals we are laying out the path for the achievement of our own goals. When we help to open doors for others, we are sowing the seeds for others to open doors for us when we need this. When we recognise and cultivate the greatness in others, we are recognising and cultivating the greatness in ourselves.

> As we help others grow, so we grow
> As we give, so we receive

Cultivating Kindness – Spreading the seeds of Empowerment

- Find 3 ways in which you can empower yourself daily
- Find 7 things you can do to help others in your business
- Think of 3 people who can help you grow – approach them
- Perform one act of random kindness daily for a month
- Consider 3 people you can add to your team with more skill than you
- Who can help you raise your game?
- How can you make it happen?

When you stand in your power and can grant others the right to stand in theirs, and when you are so aware of the combined power that is so generated that you can direct and use it, then you have a veritable 'powerhouse' at your disposal. Start to create your powerhouse today!

7. Seventh Secret of Wealth Creation – Knowing *(Holding the Space Open)*

How many wealthy people do you know of or have read about who do not follow their intuition or gut feel or sense of knowing? Yet intuition does not feature strongly in the 'how to become rich' manuals and guide books. It is truly one of the greatest secrets of wealth creation. Those who have mastered wealth creation have a sense of 'knowing'. They 'know' what to buy, what to sell, when to buy, when to sell, who to trust, who not to trust, where to go, what to do. They seem to magically pick the winning industries, trends, ideas.

And no one thinks to ask them 'how'. Their sense of 'knowing' or following their instinct, their intuition, gut, or sixth sense is so acute, that they speak of their knowing as some sort of fact. And everyone who hears them is so acutely aware of the authenticity behind their words that they too buy into the picture, never doubting it for a moment.

Do these great rainmakers get it wrong sometimes? Sure they do. But they move right along. They cut losses, sell off, make a new plan and move right on. Does a setback cause them to put their whole system of knowing into doubt? No, it does not.

Do these great rainmakers start a dream by questioning what they know? Do they ask 'How do I know this is my intuition?' or 'How can I trust this?' They do not. Yes, they will deal with facts and figures and numbers later on in the process – but to begin with, they 'know'.

Among the most frequently asked questions on my courses and one-on-one wealth alignments are: 'How do I know it's intuition?', 'How can I trust it?', 'How do I know this feeling is not leading me down some murky path?'

All this reminds me of a long distance Wealth Alignment I did over the phone last week. This lady is the major breadwinner in the family. She was seeking guidance for enormous change in her life. It would involve leaving a lucrative business grown over many years and starting afresh in a new city (which made her heart soar) in order to pursue and realise a deeply heartfelt dream. Was this logical? Could the heart and inner knowing be trusted?

After a very powerful energetic transformation, she really connected with her sense of inner knowing and power. She suddenly realised, 'I have never done anything that would harm my family before. I have never led them down the wrong path. So I am not likely to do anything now that would hurt either me or them.' That's trusting inner knowing!

> You must without-a-shadow-of-doubt know
> You must you-bet-your-bottom-dollar know
> You must absolutely know

Fortunes have been made because people trusted their inner voice over what was going on around them. Fortunes have been lost or not made because people did the opposite too. How much do you trust your 'knowing'? How much faith and store do you set by it? Witness Donald Trump, one billion dollars in debt, telling the bank he would set it right – and then doing just that.

Here I am, and two years into my writing I have two books on the shelves – *Money Alchemy* ™ which came out just less than a year ago, and *Money Well* ™ which was launched earlier this week. They are wonderful books and *I know* they will become international best-sellers! *I know* millions of copies will sell around the world. *I know* they will be translated into 19 languages. Yet as facts stand right now, international rights have not even been explored. Yet. And for a full explanation of 'Yet' you must read *The Money Well*.

But still, **I know**. I absolutely know. I without-a-shadow-of-doubt know. I you-bet-your-bottom-dollar know. Why do I know? How do I know? *I simply know.*

That is definitely one of the most powerful secrets of wealth creation. It's similar to Believe. Knowing is like an inner guiding compass, opening pathways by its presence and direction.

Because it's Knowing that solidifies and grooves-in the pathways of attainment not only into our own unconscious, but also into the collective unconscious – making it possible for others too to focus their energy on the achievement of our goal.

What does that mean? Well, when Sol Kerzner paints a beautiful, vivid, multicoloured picture of the new magical world he intends to create, long before a brick is laid down – does not everyone buy into the vision, and does not everyone's energy get directed onto the completed dream, thereby helping to make it a reality?

And can you all now see my books on all the shelves, of all the bookstores around the world, in big piles, with 'International Bestseller', and 'Oprah's List' stuck on the right hand corner? Can you see it? Can you see *Money Well*™ and *Money Alchemy*™ and *Wealth Journey*™ and *Relationship Alchemy*® in French, and German, and Italian, and Chinese, and Arabic, and Sotho? (Okay, so maybe you can't read the titles, so look for Kiki Theo – but can you see it?)

Well, thank you very much! That really helps a lot.

Do you get it?

Let's look at our sense of Knowing and reflect on how much we trust our intuition.

Reflecting on Knowing

- What do I know?
- What do I not know?
- If you don't know, who does? Why do they know?
- Think of 3 times recently when you 'just knew'? Which part of the body/head did the knowingness originate from? What kind of emotion was present?
- Think of another 3 times when you 'just knew' or had a feeling? Locate areas as above
- Reflect on your sense of knowing across time. Look for patterns, emotions, location of the thoughts and feelings
- If you knew you were right, what would you be doing right now?
- If you could trust your intuition implicitly, what would you do?

Well … What are you waiting for??

How does it feel to simply know?

Take any decisions you need to take as a result of this knowledge. Formulate a plan of action and do it. **Connect with the feel-good feeling!** *Make any changes you need to make in your life. Keep it simple. Keep it light. Keep it fun.*

Cultivating a sense of Knowing

- Look for places and situations where you can practise Knowing daily
- Acknowledge when you are right
- Listen to and follow your intuition
- Set your intent on connecting with your Knowing

- Decide to always believe in and follow your inner sense of Knowing from this day on
- Perform a symbolic act of opening up the space of Knowing

A symbolic act can take any shape or form depending on you. You could for example light a candle and speak a few words from your heart, or buy a plant or other beautiful object which you keep as a reminder of your new intent. Or you could dance around a fire at new moon. Any symbolic act done with intent will help to focus your energy and align your purpose.

Who could possibly know what you want and need better than you?
Once you know the answer to that one, the sky's the limit!

When you Know, you are holding the space of possibility open for all good things to unfold

8. Eighth Secret of Wealth Creation – Rejoice *(Celebrating Life)*

Rejoicing and celebrating our good fortune, or having a sense of deserving, or feeling gratitude or, in other words, being totally in the present moment is one of the key secrets of wealth creation. Hence, it is secret number eight, eight being the number of abundance. And I must tell you, this just 'happened', I truly did not plan it – not consciously, anyway.

Rejoicing – celebrating, being happy – is not generally encouraged or cultivated in our world. Think about it. Sure, you're allowed to have a few moments here and there, perhaps at graduation, a wedding (where crying is also encouraged) or a birth. But, as a general trend, we look askance at people who seem too happy, or who laugh too much. We become embarrassed even, when others are so brimming with excitement and well-being that we cannot help but smile – because laughter and joy are contagious.

We are extremely cautious around joy, we traipse around it tentatively, afraid we might 'catch it' like some sort of virus. Have you ever driven or walked around smiling to yourself and then noticed how stressed people look when you glance in their direction, sometimes inadvertently? Try it. See how most people scowl and quickly look away, or they look around to see if it's someone else you are casting your joy towards. They give you that 'Don't you *dare* give me some of *that!*' look. Then they look down and scurry away. Fast. Before the joy gets them too.

Money and its flow is a light and fun resonance

Comedy features very minutely in entertainment, advertising and the media. Consider how much movie, theatre, book, art, music, soapie, advert, email, newspaper, and even talk – time is devoted to fun and joy? As compared with: *pain ~ suffering ~ angst ~ violence ~ destruction ~ war ~ crime ~ dreadful futures ~ moaning, groaning and complaining ~ running someone or something down ~ illness ~ death ~ possibility of illness and death ~ insurance against illness and death ~ engineered illness and death ~ relationship trauma, drama, divorce, heartbreak and more suffering ~ litigation ~ abandonment ~ angst over image ~ weight loss trauma ~ weight gain trauma ~ make-overs ~ bad teeth ~ body odour ~ indigestion ~ deception ~ drug use and abuse ~ earthquakes ~ tsunamis and other acts of God ~ hell, damnation and fear of God ~ terrorism ~ genocide ~ conspiracies and prophecies about the end of time.*

How do you feel just reading those words? Consider that the above forms the subject matter of the majority of our so called 'entertainment' – our movies, videos, art, music, books, theatre. Consider how little input we get which is enlivening, enlightening, fun, or joyful. Consider how little talk and encouragement we get to rejoice, to lighten up, to celebrate. Consider how we are not encouraged in any way to check our happiness levels.

We have no lessons on how to contain joy, happiness or laughter. No pointers on how to laugh louder, better, more regularly. No subject at school that correlates future job possibilities against how much joy these create in our being. No instruction on developing a sense of well-being. There are no adverts that highlight the benefits to health of celebrating. No insurance premium deduction for having a high score in childlike exuberance, no medical aid bonus for regular rejoicing.

By far the majority of parents do not raise us to pursue joy. They do not assess potential husbands and wives in terms of how much their presence raises our thriller index – on the contrary, the happier and more in love we appear to be, the more we are told to beware, as joy will not last. Parents do not encourage or sponsor the education that will make us happiest – they direct us towards aptitude, family business, or the big buck.

So it is no small wonder that we grow up being wary of happiness, distrustful of joy, half welcoming it into our lives with only one hand while the other hand holds the door open, waiting for joy's quick departure.

As a subject, rejoicing is confined to Evangelical religious groups, very young children who 'don't know better', the Dalai Lama, and the certifiably insane. Laughter and happiness, something we all yearn for so much, is the thing we probably pay the least attention to in terms of time, effort, and cultivation.

REJOICE! LAUGH!

When last did you wake up in the morning with the intent of laughing as much possible that day? When did 'lack of joy' feature as a reason for not accepting a high-paying job? When last did you do something for the simple reason that it gave you joy? When did you last enjoy the sunset or sunrise? When last were you happy for no reason whatsoever? When last did you REJOICE! LAUGH! Have fun?

Yet we are told that rejoicing is a vital part of our connection to the Divine and to self. We are encouraged to be joyful and to celebrate in all the various religions and paths – or at least to be content. Because contentment is the foundation of joy – the sort of joy that wells up from the inside, the sort of joy that is not dependent on external events.

Rejoicing is a very high frequency, a very light frequency. And we need light and fun in order to fly. We need light and fun in order to create wealth because money and its flow is a light and fun resonance.

So, let us *thrill ~ be excited ~ exult ~ rejoice ~ be totally joyous over good news ~ celebrate the good fortune of others ~ share kind deeds ~ circulate songs of joy ~ write letters of praise ~ send out cards of gratitude ~ bask in the sunlight ~ be thrilled with the moon and stars ~ chuckle ~ giggle ~ snigger ~ snort ~ cackle ~ chortle ~ hoot ~ get wound up over life's many opportunities ~ elaborate on dreams ~ create unheard of new realities ~ imagine positive outcomes ~ connect with the feel-good feeling ~ greet the divinity in others ~ love a challenge ~ enjoy making a phone call*

~ throw a party ~ enumerate the beauty of a new day ~ look for opportunities ~ spot the many doors that open each day ~ get ecstatic when you see him/her ~ seize the day! ~ expand your radiance ~ light up the room with your smile ~ shake what your mamma gave you ~ twinkle ~ glitter ~ use glitter ~ tickle yourself pink ~ laugh ~ laugh ~ laugh!

Let's look at Rejoicing and reflect on how much we celebrate life.

Reflecting on Rejoicing

- What gives me joy? How often do I do it?
- What makes me laugh? How often do I do it?
- What do I like doing for fun? How often do I do it?
- When did I last celebrate life?
- When last did I celebrate the sunrise? The sunset? The colour of the sky? The moon?
- What do I rejoice in?
- What am I grateful for in my life?
- What do I need to celebrate?

How does it feel to be joyful?

Take any decisions you need to take as a result of this knowledge. Formulate a plan of action and do it. **Connect with the feel-good feeling!** *Make any changes you need to make in your life. Keep it simple. Keep it light. Keep it fun.*

Cultivating a sense of Celebration – Being Happy!

How to do it? Well the Buddhists say, 'If you want to be happy, be happy'. First and foremost it's a decision. Because of the lack of attention paid to discovering our own unique components of joy, most of us do not know what we want or need to be happy. Every now and again, by some or other fluke, some adrenalin gets released and we feel 'happy' – often while intoxicated in some way. We then believe that this is joy.

Some of us then get hooked on continuous stimulus for the production of this 'happiness' and we are teaching our children to do the same. This, in my opinion, is the real cause behind the so called attention deficit disorder that seems suddenly to be afflicting the affluent children in the world. Less affluent children simply cannot afford the enormous amount of sensory stimulation (constant TV, video games, cellphone, ipod and other equipment, masses of chemicals and sugar, stress and performance anxiety) required to so overload energy circuits that 'attention deficit' results. In reality, the child is simply trying to get away from massive sensory overload.

If you want to be happy, be happy

External stimulus cannot produce joy. Joy does not come from the outside. Joy and happiness are not the *result* of something. But even as I see you all nod in agreement to that – yes, we all know 'happiness comes from the inside' – the way to go about bringing that happiness out is not always very clear.

The key is to practise. Being happy requires practice. Like piano playing, tennis playing, gossip mongering, whingeing, money-making, depression, spreading joy, making others feel good, disempowering people, leading, good salesmanship, patience, gracefulness, enthusiasm, being funny, being bitchy, empowering people, being aggressive, trusting, being kind. It all requires practice.

It's quite something to think about, isn't it? Because we

think people are born nice, not nice, happy, sad, depressed, with a gift to spread joy or not, aggressive, or plain old miserable. Consider for a moment how much effort it takes to cultivate these qualities, to deeply entrench them into one's being. Consider that the more you bitch, the bitchier you become. The more you whine, the whinier you become. The more you practise aggression, the more aggressive you become. The more you encourage people, the more inspirational you become. The more you are kind, the kinder you become. The more you spread good news, the better you make the world.

More importantly – the more you smile, the happier you become. The more you rejoice, the more rejoicefull you become – and there is apparently no such word as rejoicefull, my computer says, underlining the word in red. And yet we should be cultivating rejoicefulness and happyfullness (not exactly the same as happiness actually). We should be funfully employed (I'm going for a sentencefull...), we should be laughterfully married. We should spread celebratory news and we should engage a meaningful portion of each day in the pursuit of pure silliness.

Money will surely follow. But if it doesn't, we'll at least be happy. What price can you put on that? Happiness is a decision. Decide today you will be happy. Practise being happy. Remove things from your life (books, magazines, newspapers, TV programmes, art, music) that do not add to joy and happiness. Surround yourself with people and things that add to your joy. Spread joy. Spread good news. Bury bad news, rumours, gossip (unless it's good), and negative predictions. Spread good news (I repeat). See my creategoodnews.com website.

Cultivating a Happyfull, Rejoicefull, Joyfull Life!

- Take the decision to rejoice daily
- Set time aside daily to have fun – find what that means for you
- Laugh – 3x daily – find a way to do it
- Make it a priority to celebrate something weekly – could be the beauty of a rose
- Count your blessings – out loud
- Count your blessings – on paper
- Count your blessings while showering in the morning in a silly voice
- Sing your blessings!
- Sing praises to God, the sunset, the moon, your children, your cellphone
- Give thanks where it is needed
- Pay 3 compliments daily
- Connect with a feel-good joyful space inside and spread it outside
- Hug a tree
- Hug another tree where someone can see you
- Give a gift of kindness to someone each day
- Dance with your dog or cat
- Wear a silly hat or outfit at least once a month
- Celebrate with someone you love – that could be you

Basically, all everyone wants is to be happy. No one actually wants money, not really. That's quite a thought, because once you master knowing and finding your joy – the rest will simply follow. That is what is truly meant by 'Seek ye first the kingdom of God'.

Being happy requires practise
Being happy is a decision

9. Ninth Secret of Wealth Creation – Create *(Imagining Reality)*

Wealth creators are the dream merchants of our world. They invent fabulous new realities. They reconfigure the future. They challenge the very nature of what is real and possible. They dream. And those dreams are so infused with Presence, Belief, Authority, Daring, Knowing, and Rejoicing that reality shifts around to accommodate them. Wealth follows. Really read that paragraph again.

Creators of wealth are constantly creating, constantly dreaming, constantly believing. And once one dream is turned into reality, they create another. They do not stop the cycle of give and receive, just as nature does not stop creating. The universe is endlessly abundant, forever growing, forever flourishing, then falling back, summer to winter, and the cycle begins again. To stop is to perish.

Highly successful people from any field never retire. Great businessmen and women, renowned authors, skilled musicians, superior sportsmen, prima ballerinas, child prodigies, the cream of dress designers, seasoned Oscar winners – never retire. They are too busy creating. They need to create. Their very nature is creation.

And from creation, more creation follows. When we stop dreaming the future we die. Dreaming implies hoping, it implies change and our willingness to embrace it. Creating implies taking responsibility, and our willingness to do that. Creating and dreaming are positive acts of expansion of self.

We are always creating – by word, thought or deed; by

adding our energy and attention to the creations of others; or by withholding our energy and attention from the creation of others. We are constantly, with our every breath and thought, co-creating our world moment by moment. We create joy, misery, pain, suffering, happiness, expansion, poverty, wealth. We create health, disease, wars, peace, pollution, and preservation. It is in our nature to create. It is in our nature to dream. That is why we have minds and emotions. That is why we are made of energy. And most importantly, that is why we are aware of being made of energy. That is why we are aware of being aware.

So if we are to create something, if we are to dream something, if we are to add our energy and thought and attention to something – let that something be beautiful, let it be wholesome, let it be expansive, let it be constructive. Let it make the world a better place. We have the choice. Let us exercise it well. That is known as consciousness.

Reflecting on Creation

- What do I create daily with my words, thoughts, deeds?
- What do I add my energy and attention to?
- What do I dream?
- How do I shape the future?
- What is my vision of the future?
- Which dreams does my energy fuel?
- What new reality am I willing to create?

How does it feel to be dreaming a new reality?

Take any decisions you need to take as a result of this knowledge. Formulate a plan of action and do it. **Connect with the feel-good feeling!** *Make any changes you need to make in your life. Keep it simple. Keep it light. Keep it fun.*

Cultivating the Art of Co-creation – Imagining new Realities

So many years ago now, John Lennon wrote a song called 'Imagine'. It was a very profound song which invited the listener to contemplate a totally new reality, a new world. His words are as relevant today as they were then, and as they always will be in the future.

What can *you* imagine? How much time and energy do you spend each day working on your future, your wealth, your dreams, the future of the world – in your imagination? Most successful people from businessmen to sportsmen to artists spend considerable time dreaming their new realities. They create their vision in their head first – whether it's a new property, a restaurant, or winning a race. First they create it energetically in the land of dreams. They infuse that creation with deep emotion. They work out all the details very specifically – the shapes, colours, forms, numbers, people – everything involved. Not the details of how to do it, but the details of the completed creation, the completed dream. (That is a very important detail.)

Successful creators do not start by trying to figure out the 'how' of their creation – they simply work on the completed creation itself. First they imagine it, in spectacular detail. They dream it, feel it, be it, they work on the completed dream itself.

What can you imagine?

Many people will not imagine. They will not create new realities. They stop before they start because their mind throws 'how?' at them. They do not Trust, Dare, or Believe. They do not Know, so they will not Challenge.

What can you imagine?

As I sit here writing today, in my little studio, we have builders renovating the French doors leading from the studios to the long veranda overlooking the Kalk Bay harbour. They have been here for weeks. They are a total disruption. They do their work completely unconscious of people like me sitting here trying to write. Apart from the noise necessary in drilling and cutting and grinding, they smoke and joke and talk to people in the street down below in loud voices. They jostle with one another, rolling around on the veranda floor, and play music loudly on their cellphones. All with total and absolute lack of awareness or interest in the tenants trying to work. It is highly annoying. But as I sit here writing, one part of my mind is imagining.

What am I imagining? I am imagining a course for builders and their staff, a training in building etiquette that will put the workers' awareness on the people around the building, minimising disruption. I imagine telling the owner of the building company that this will increase production. That people who have had a pleasant experience will tell others. This is what I imagine. I will probably never deliver such a course. But I cannot help imagining it. It is a habit of mine, looking at how to make things better, how to add value. It's what I do. And the fact that I am doing it, the fact that I imagine this, is helping to create this reality even as I write. Probably by the time this book is out, someone, somewhere, will be training builders in building etiquette – if they are not doing it already.

In fact, now that I think about it, there are all sorts of other worker-related etiquette courses one could teach plumbers, electricians, and all sorts of repair-type people. Starting with how to wipe shoes on the way into a house, to where to put down tools and tool boxes and where not to, to where (or rather how) not to smoke, and so on. Of course there are many repair-type people with impeccable manners and etiquette. Especially in Switzerland.

The point is that when you leave the doors of imagination open, opportunity, creation, and money can come in.

Cultivating Imagination – Remembering to Dream

- What can you imagine?
- Create your ideal dream of the future
- Write a list of far out solutions for some global problems
- Read some fantasy fiction
- Look for fairies in the garden – really look
- Invent something
- Look for spaceships in the sky – even if you don't believe they're there, look
- Imagine your ideal life
- Imagine being wealthy

If you cannot imagine it, who will?

10. Tenth Secret of Wealth Creation – Deliver *(Cultivating Will)*

You've got to DO IT! That's the bottom line. Wealth creators do it. (Birds do it, bees do it ... it's important to stay light.) Wealth creators do it. They deliver. At the end of the day, as well as at the beginning and the middle, you have to Do It. That's all it ultimately boils down to. You can Imagine, Know, Believe, Trust, Rejoice, and Challenge till the cows come home, but if you don't deliver it's all meaningless.

Delivering means keeping your word, doing what you say you will do, being dependable and reliable. It means that others see you as a good bet. It means that you have so integrated the secrets of Imagine and Confront and Challenge and Know and Trust and Dare and Believe that you emanate these qualities. Others believe your dream too. They are willing to bet on you, because they know you will deliver.

You've got to DO IT!
That's the bottom line

I believe in delivery, so I deliver. I add value. And it's not so much a matter of what I do as of who I am. Delivery is a part of me – maybe I was born with the inclination, it's certainly been well honed and cultivated over decades. I am almost incapable of shoddiness or incompletion – no matter what the circumstances. I find it near impossible – no, change that to *impossible* – to do a half job.

And this I think accounts for much of my success in the business world. For when I approached buyers at construction companies in my late teens offering them a 24-hour power tool sale and repair service, and undertaking to do better for them than the power tool agents with whom they had been dealing for years, they believed me.

And when, in my mid twenties, I approached very wealthy individuals and offered to increase the returns on their equity investments, they believed me – despite my age, sex, lack of relevant education or reputation, inexperience, newly formed company with no track record, and lack of tangible assets of my own.

So what were these clients buying, and why? They were mostly men, much older, wiser, wealthier and more experienced than myself. I had very little to offer in terms of the usual things we measure – experience, track record, education. Even in terms of physical appearance I was somewhat lacking – small, dark haired, short, even in high heeled shoes. Not a cover-girl contender by any stretch of the imagination.

What people really buy is your ability to deliver

Why would highly successful individuals, then, potentially put at risk (not the price of a pair of shoes, or even a car) hundreds of thousands, in many cases millions, of hard-earned cash by dealing with me? This was retirement money, savings, investments, which, due to the nature of the stock exchange, could have been halved overnight with incompetent decision making. So why were these clients buying from me? And what were they actually buying?

What they were buying was my ability to deliver. They were buying the fact that my word is my bond. They were buying my total belief in my ability to add value. They were buying my absolute conviction that no one would care better for them than I would. (They were also buying their sound decision making ability.) And their decision to deal with me was sound indeed. Because I did deliver, I did add value, I did make money for my clients – who were indeed older and wiser, just as I said.

All this is implied and contained in that little word: delivery. What people really buy is your ability to deliver. And your ability to deliver is a resonance which you exude when you are steeped in it enough – just like some people exude charisma, or leadership, or comfort.

Delivery is one of the cornerstones of the wealth creation process. It is indeed one of the greatest secrets because it's no secret at all – therefore most people underestimate its value and its existence – or they fluff over it.

Do you deliver? Can you say, I *WILL* deliver, no matter what?

Reflecting on Delivery

- Can I be totally relied upon to deliver?
- Who/what do I blame for non-delivery?
- Is my word my bond?
- How can I improve my delivery?
- List any incomplete delivery in your life – complete it

How does it feel to know you will always deliver, no matter what?

Take any decisions you need to take as a result of this knowledge. Formulate a plan of action and do it. **Connect with the feel-good feeling!** *Make any changes you need to make in your life. Keep it simple. Keep it light. Keep it fun.*

Cultivating the Will – The key to Delivery

As I sit here, still writing at 14h30 on a Friday afternoon, my body is tiring and the sunny day and sparkly sea beckon. I have been writing since 9h00 this morning with a short break and stroll combined for lunch. Now my shoulders and neck ache, and my head is full and calling for me to wrap up the day – since the start of the previous section, in fact. But I am exercising my will. I decided this morning to go all the way to the end of Secret number 11. So I will do it. Perhaps these chapters will be rather short, but I will do it ...

Doing what you say you will do, delivering no matter what,

is a question of habit, and of will. Cultivating the will takes practice. It involves pushing limits and boundaries and those limits and boundaries first exist in the mind. We stretch the mind by stretching ourselves. I am stretching myself sitting here writing. It would be far easier to go home, or to go for a swim. (And remember, I don't even have a boss ...)

We stretch the mind by Imagining, by cultivating Belief and Knowing, by delivering a bit more than we need to, by going that extra bit beyond what is comfortable. Athletes and high performers of all kind train to do this, and it's a very definite part of wealth training too.

When you routinely stretch yourself, it becomes the norm, it becomes part of your practice, and it serves to cultivate the belief that anything is possible. Can I finish this section? Yes. Okay, how about I do it before 16h00? Now *that's a stretch!* But why not? I'm game! So I go for that. Maybe if I work it out in words per minute it's not physically possible, but if I believe it can happen, then it will.

When you play with stretching, the universe will stretch with you too. When you make magic happen in your daily life, magic will happen in your daily life.

When your mind expands, your money expands also

Cultivating Will – Stretching the mind

- Decide to do everything with 10% more effort
- Do some ordinary tasks in half the time
- When you are totally finished, carry on for another half hour
- Set yourself some tasks and complete them
- Give up something, for practice – chocolate, tea, TV

- Do 3 things you would normally avoid
- Take some decisions and execute them
- Decide to increase your wealth (why else are you reading this book?)

When you deliver, the universe, which is only a reflection of you, will deliver also. It is (verily) not the universe that delivers, but you!

11. Eleventh Secret of Wealth Creation – Be(come) *(Transforming Self)*

The wealth creation journey is first and foremost a journey of becoming; it is a journey of transformation of self, it is a journey of transcending. It is the search for our humanity and the recognition of the Divine that lives within us all.

When we set out to discover self, whichever way we may go about it, we try out different versions of becoming. We experiment with our bodies – thin, boyish, curvy, buxom, sexy. We try different looks – happy-go-lucky, dangerous, sultry, tall-dark-and-handsome, Peter-Pan-ish, conservation-greeny, spiritual, artistic, corporate. These looks come with accompanying attitude, feelings, ways of talking and living in the world. Then we enter various groups – school, work, sport, dance, club, social – we amend our look-speech-attitude-talk-being to resonate with these also.

We make adjustments in our beingness for parents, lovers, husbands, wives, children, our race, colour, culture, religion. Then we are impacted by life experience; media – lots of media; advertising – a serious amount of it; the material we read, and see, and listen to.

And then we ask 'Who am I?', 'What do I want?', 'Where

am I going?' And we have absolutely no idea. And who can blame us?

> You are never as much in your power as you are
> when you are deeply and profoundly being Just You

Many people want money so they can feel free to express and be who they really are (or think they are). Many people create wealth so they can do as they please with no interference, so they no longer need to conform or please anyone, so they can be true to themselves.

We all yearn to be truly ourselves. Yet we spend much of our lives trying to be like others. We try to dress, or talk, or even think like those around us. While deep down inside we yearn to be authentic – just the way we were created to be.

The search for authenticity is a search for power. For you are never as much in your power as you are when you are deeply and profoundly being Just You. On some level we all know that. And it's a strange conundrum too. Because the sooner we accept who we are, the sooner we come into our power, the sooner the world opens up to us and the sooner we will acquire our heart's desire. But we generally think it's the other way around.

We think once we have acquired our heart's desire, we will be free to be who we are. End the struggle now. You can never truly be anyone but yourself. Start the practice of being you today.

Being is, indeed, one of the great secrets of wealth creation. Successful wealth creators are usually very distinctive – they stand out because they have truly cultivated and embraced themselves fully – warts and all, as they say. They stand out from the crowd because they highlight and enhance their differences. They rejoice in their peculiarities. They have integrated all the qualities we have discussed in the first ten secrets of wealth creation which are also the secrets of self creation. Cultivating Presence through Confront. Awakening through Challenge. Opening the Heart by Believing. Developing Daring. Cultivating Authority. Sowing Kindness. Knowing. Celebrating Life. Creating, Dreaming, Imagining. Cultivating Will.

So who are you? And are you willing to become yourself?

Reflecting on Beingness

- Who am I? (Ask this 11x while looking in the mirror)
- Who is ....? (Insert your name here)
- What makes me unique in all the world? (DNA is not the correct answer)
- How am I different from everyone else?
- Why would I love me?
- What are my unique talents and gifts?
- What am I better at than anyone else I know?
- How does it feel to be me?
- What would the world lose if I was gone?
- How can I make a difference?
- What is my purpose?
- What do I absolutely love doing?
- How can I serve?
- What stops me being me?
- What do I love about myself?
- What needs transforming?
- What peculiarities and quirkiness do I exhibit?
- What 'negative' qualities in me am I willing to accept?
- Why am I absolutely wonderful?

How does it feel to be absolutely, totally, over the top ME?

Take any decisions you need to take as a result of this knowledge. Formulate a plan of action and do it. **Connect with the feel-good feeling!** *Make any changes you need to make in your life. Keep it simple. Keep it light. Keep it fun.*

Cultivating Beingness – Allowing Self to Emerge

- Spend some time every day with yourself
- Do the things you love
- Decide now not to try and change who you are for anyone
- Celebrate your you-ness daily
- Affirm your uniqueness and individuality in every way you can
- Commit to honouring your truth
- Speak your mind
- Do only what feels right for you
- Follow your bliss
- Pray for guidance
- Sit quietly daily and commune with the quiet voice within
- Celebrate being you!

Yes, I have finished – though it's now a quarter to five. But now, I will stretch just a little further by finishing off the summary too. What a superstar!

The 11 Secrets of Wealth Creation are keys to unlocking not only wealth but also relationships, life and self. By cultivating each one, you integrate qualities that will enable you to complete any journey successfully. However, from time to time you will be tested, and these tests manifest as detours along your path.

In the next section we will deal with these Wealth Detours – those things that may take you away from your path to wealth and learn how to get back on the track to wealth.

5

Why You Are Still Not There

Transforming the 9 Wealth Detours

1. Excuses
2. Patterns
3. Specialness
4. Greed
5. Complication
6. Ambiguity
7. Procrastination
8. Illusion
9. Fear

The 9 Wealth Challenges are repeated here so you can cross-reference the detours as necessary:

1. Avoidance : Confront   Key: Courage   Root: Perseverance
2. Denial : Responsibility Key: Truth   Root: Honour
3. Struggle : Embrace   Key: Flow   Root: Allow
4. Control : Expand   Key: Generosity   Root: Openness
5. Complicate: Simplify   Key: Choice   Root: Knowledge
6. Dissipate : Contain   Key: Purpose   Root: Service
7. Daydream : Create   Key: Action   Root: Grounding
8. Dictate : Direct   Key: Vision   Root: Clarity
9. Power : Transcend   Key: Appreciate   Root: Divine
                                              Connection

Each level of Wealth Consciousness and every Wealth Challenge has an inbuilt wealth detour which, if taken, can misdirect you along the path to wealth, away from your course and purpose. Although each detour correlates with the levels of Wealth Consciousness and Wealth Challenges, as with all the other elements of this Wealth Consciousness model, the detours can also present on any level along the Wealth Journey. So, for example, although Greed is a detour which is very obviously present at the level of Dependence, where Control – Expansion is being transcended into Generosity, Greed can present as a detour anywhere along the path. At the level of Wealth, for instance, Greed can misdirect you away from Affluence.

The holographic nature of the Wealth Journey model allows for some or all of the detours to present between one level of Wealth Consciousness and another. By integrating and using the qualities of each wealth challenge, we are able to get back on track from a detour.

Wealth detours take us off course along our Wealth Journey

and in our lives. They pose as one thing, whereas they are another. The wealth detours represent nothing more than fear of change. All the wealth detours are manifestations of ego grasping – the ego does not want to relinquish control.

The key thing about a detour is recognition and awareness. We need to recognise, as soon as possible, that we are off track and get back on to the road to wealth.

1. First Wealth Detour – EXCUSES
– *Why it's better not to grow*
– Sharpen your Will

Many people never embark on the Wealth Journey because they are too busy looking for reasons not to. They will tell you why they don't need much money, how they cannot advertise because they 'just couldn't', how someone's brother's, auntie's second cousin was filthy rich but such a total miser ('what's the point of that?'), how they're okay (mostly), how they have no problem making money, but they love to spend (giggle, giggle), and then they may move on to talking about the evil-money-mongering corporations which destroy the planet, radical socio-economic barter systems, sustainable economies, and how 'the ongoing decline in economic growth is the precursor for a move from abstract to concrete economic values signalling the end of the economic cycle in accordance with the predictions of the Mayan calendar'. And all that because I happened to say, at a brunch one day, 'I write books on wealth creation.' I kid you not.

We are raised on excuses for being poor, or if not exactly poor, then not quite wealthy – and certainly not mega-rich. We are fed religious, moral and creative grounds on which to prefer, if not exactly poverty, then some sort of mediocrity in the wealth department. We are prepared (by the many good books) to be able to withstand, tolerate, and even rejoice, should abject poverty actually be inflicted upon us.

The world is a bountiful place filled with pure energy – you can create as much money as you like in it

In all the years I have been writing and teaching and coaching on wealth creation, I have not once heard someone say, 'Well, my mother taught me to love money', or 'I remember my father blessing money and rejoicing every time he got to pay his taxes', or 'I was taught at a young age to do a little dance of joy when I was given my pocket money'. Never, not once, have I heard these words come out of anyone's lips. Have you?

Did anyone ever tell you that the world is a bountiful place filled with pure energy and that you can create as much money as you like in it? Or that you should go forth and do what gives you a thrill, enjoy life, have fun, celebrate, and make lots and lots of cash? That you deserve and are entitled to abundance? Did a single one of your teachers, parents, relatives, guardians, or friends ever tell you anything like that? ... Mine neither.

So we have a culture of excuse-mongerers (another word the dictionary does not like), who train us, from very early on, how to avoid expansion (even as we are, in the same breath, commanded to excel). We are given the words and the rules and the pictures that create our prison of excuses. And it is these excuses that keep us from moving forward, and take us away from our path to wealth.

Some people never start the Wealth Journey because of these excuses. Others begin, and at the first opportunity fall back on their excuses as a way of not moving forward or carrying things through. Excuses can create a detour at any and every step along the Wealth Consciousness levels and at every point along the wealth challenges, cancelling your gains and making you forget your purpose.

The best remedy is to take a decision, right now, *for life,* that goes:

NO EXCUSES. Absolutely NO EXCUSES

For what? For anything, anywhere, anytime. If you can make that firm commitment now, it will be the metaphorical equivalent of fitting yourself with roller blades for your Wealth Journey. Or maybe a jet plane.

'No excuses' means you'll get the job done, *no matter what.* It means you will persist and you will continue, *no matter what.* And let's examine the *no matter what* and what constitutes it or, in other words, the nature of our excuses.

By far the greatest culprit is this thing called 'logic', which encompasses all manner of excuses that have been 'logically', and particularly 'quantifiably', and most especially 'statistically' verified by rational, logical, scientific people, economists, bankers, and others who 'know more and know better'.

I won't go into how you can prove anything 'logically' if you know the rules; or how a teensy, tiny, infinitesimally small number of people cannot and never will represent the whole – which is in any case always greater than the sum of its parts. Nor how the observer affects that which is observed (which has now been 'scientifically proven'), and which is an oxymoron of really special note.

No, what I will comment on, is that when someone says, as someone was saying at a recent dinner, that 'this will be the worst quarter ever for retailers' and that 'the retail industry is down 40%' and that 'no one is buying anything', the (untrained) rational mind, because its thinking is very linear and therefore very limited, will think something like this: Every shop in every shopping centre throughout the country (in fact throughout the world ... this is called extrapolating) is selling 40% less than they were before. No one is buying. Therefore 'every' shop owner is not making a profit. Therefore 'everyone' is running at a loss. This is called a statistic.

Now if I say, 'But many people in retail are making lots of money too', economists will shoot me down (as did those at the brunch). Reality however is in no way linear. And in actual fact, there will be those retailers whose sales are down 10%, others who will be down 60%, and some who will be up 30% too. And if you think about it, even for a little moment, you cannot help but see the 'logic' in this argument. The real question, though, is: Which reality will you align yourself with?

And the answer always has to be, and always must be: That reality which empowers me and helps me to expand. End of chat.

Whether it's a question of 'recession', conspiracy theory, advice, statistics, or the choice of lipstick, ask yourself if it expands or shrinks you. Follow, align with, believe, put energy into, trust, only that which expands and empowers.

Now excuses don't generally do that. Excuses generally give you a reason to shrink. Don't do it.

NO EXCUSES. Absolutely NO EXCUSES. Just DO IT!

Nothing exists in isolation on this planet, and everything is always in a state of balance. So always remember, whenever there is a lack of some sort somewhere, there is a great abundance somewhere else to make up for it. That is universal law. And that is truth (or 'a' truth anyway).

The Excuses detour correlates with the Wealth Challenge of Avoidance – Confront. While you are embroiled in excuses you avoid, and you cannot confront. Excuses relates to the Wealth Consciousness of Ignorance. For while you entertain, believe, and encourage excuses, you remain uninformed. And, more importantly, you are not aligned with either your options or your power. Excuses close doors before they can even open.

Excuses can present as a detour anywhere along the Wealth Consciousness scale or along the Wealth Challenges. The excuses just become more sophisticated and less easy to spot for what they are as you progress further along the wealth path. All excuses are based on fear and on the inability or unwillingness to confront and to change.

When an excuse takes you off the path to wealth – *no matter what* it is : a 'down turn' in the economy, fierce competitors, loss of energy, illness, a setback, doubt, fear, more doubt and fear, sharpen your WILL and commit.

As soon as you realise you are off on a detour, get back on track. Focus your intent. Tighten up your will, and DO IT!! No Excuses.

Inspired Action:	*Align with that which expands*
	Drop your excuses
	Focus your intent
	Tighten up your Will
	DO IT!

Commitment: 'I will persist until I succeed for that is the secret of success in all ventures' (from Og Mandino's *Greatest salesman in the world*)

2. Second Wealth Detour – PATTERNS
– *The cause for not growing*
– Create a new groove

The second wealth detour which correlates quite obviously with the Wealth Consciousness of Blame is Patterns and it highlights the integration of the wealth challenge of Denial – Accept through Responsibility.

Often, we believe someone else is to blame for our lack of success. This happens not only at the very start of the Wealth Consciousness journey where we need to transcend Blame in order to move forward, but it also offers itself as a detour at every level along our wealth path.

What happens in real life is that somewhere along the wealth path we hit a snag which reactivates some past angst, trauma, failure, or pattern. When this happens, our energy unplugs from the present, and from our purpose, and from our commitment and focus, and it plugs instead into this old, unsuccessful, traumatic pattern which we then reactivate, replay, reconnect to, try to unravel, and eventually land up re-creating. (Don't you just hate when that happens?)

What is at the core of this detour is a desire to blame. Patterns are a different version of the Excuses detour. It is definitely an attempt to shirk responsibility. It's like a parable you may have heard of which goes something like this:

I am walking down the road when I fall into a hole. The hole is very deep and very dark. I am very unhappy and depressed. I become angry wondering, 'Why me?', 'What did I do to deserve this?', 'Why me?', 'Who left this hole here?', thinking, 'It's their fault'. I am in the hole for a very long time. Eventually, I get out.

The next day, I am walking along the same road, when I fall into the same hole. I can't believe it! The hole is very deep and very dark, and now I am even angrier and more frustrated than before. I ask myself 'Why me?', 'Why does this always happen to me?', 'What did I do to deserve this?', thinking,'It's definitely those builders, it's their fault', 'But why is it always me?' It takes a very long time to climb out. Eventually, I get out.

The next day, same thing: Same road, same hole, fall in, huge angst, big blame till I get out.

The next day, I take another road.

That's exactly the thing to do with this detour – don't go there, take another road. It's good to see the pattern. It's good to find and acknowledge and recognise the pattern. It's good to observe quite objectively and dispassionately, to reflect – looking to see only what is there. 'Ah,' you may say, 'I see that every time I employ a redhead, I become distracted and lose focus, and we go into debt.' Here comes a redhead looking for a job, and she's perfect for it, has all the qualifications, but ... 'I will not repeat the pattern. I will employ a blonde.' Make a choice. Take another road.

Or you may have recognised a pattern of crashing just as things start to come together, and on closer investigation you notice that you always go on a (very justifiable) spending spree to upgrade the office/machinery/your stationery, at this point. Choose not to do it. Take another road.

Or perhaps it's always something 'out there', something 'out of your control' – like the economy, or suppliers, or someone 'letting you down'. Choose not to go there. Take another road. *The Money Well*™ – *How to Contain Wealth* provides lots of wonderful ways in which to discover and transform patterns of this kind.

To change a pattern, you have to do something new: create

a new pattern. The mind loves to habituate. It's like the creation of a pathway in the countryside. The more you tread a path, the more it becomes grooved in. So create a different path and groove that in instead.

Learn to tell the signs of an upcoming Pattern detour. Know yourself – know your patterns.

A light task: Discover the recurring pattern in
                        your wealth, relationships, life.
                        Write it, draw it, dance it, reflect on it.

Inspired Action: *Create some new patterns*
                        Focus your intent on travelling the new
                        paths
                        Get back on track

Commitment: I will only travel the paths I choose with clear intent

3. Third Wealth Detour – SPECIALNESS – 'First I have to save the world' – Becoming Extra-Ordinary

We are all unique. We are all special. And I believe we are all here to grow and add value to ourselves, others and the world. So bear that in mind as I expand on this wealth detour.

Specialness – the dictionary wants me to say Special ness – but this is my book, and my Wealth Consciousness model so … Specialness, is a condition that afflicts many, causing them to detour not only away from wealth, but also away from life itself.

Specialness does correlate with the Wealth Consciousness of Struggle, because it is believed by those on this particular wealth detour that Struggle is the mark of Specialness itself. This thinking is the result of mass conditioning over centuries that most of us have bought into. Let's do a quick check on this.

How many of you believe that great musical talent and poverty go together? Do you believe that being an artist is a lucrative career? How about being a writer? Would you say to someone who is keen to save the whales, 'Yes! What a wonderful idea, there's a lot of money to be made in doing good for the planet.' Do you think that should be the case?

Do you think whale researchers should be as wealthy as dress designers?

Do you think social workers dealing with uplifting the lives of women and children should be as wealthy as investment bankers?

Do you believe that spiritual leaders who are holding the space for the enlightenment of others should be as wealthy as movie stars?

Should our taxes go into funding prisons, or organisations that plant trees?

Do you think organisations 'doing good' should make a profit?

Of course this is the topic for a whole new book. And it's well worth considering these questions, not only because they point to such fundamental flaws in our thinking, but because it is mind and consciousness expanding to do so.

We generally believe that anyone doing anything meaningful, life-enhancing, consciousness-expanding, creative, instructive, and in particular life-saving, should be, if not poverty-stricken, then at least barely surviving. We believe this. And we perpetuate the myth by offering (and accepting) the lowest wages and remuneration, and in many cases no wages or remuneration, for some of the most important jobs on the planet.

We cannot do great things, we can only do little things with great love.

(Mother Teresa)

Again, rate the relative importance of, say, a nurse and an economist. The one ensures a living being remains alive and recovers after an illness or accident, the other offers opinion on non-tangible mental constructs. Ouch! Who should be paid ten times more than whom?

What about a (genuine) spiritual leader and a (genuinely good) politician – shouldn't they both be driven in limousines? Shouldn't they both wear Armani? I see you shaking your heads. If not, why not?

Why is it more important to shuffle money (that does not exist) around, than it is to ensure that a whole species is not brought to extinction, thereby threatening the delicate balance of an entire planet? Even (maybe especially) if that species is a butterfly. Why should a company making shoes deserve to make a profit above a company creating homes for the homeless?

Now you may think that it is I who have taken a detour here, but I have not. I am pointing out some very genuine misconceptions in much of our thinking. And where this creates a wealth detour is that many people have so identified with this type of thinking that they cannot and, in some cases, will not make money. These folk (very brave and well meaning) somehow believe that making money (beyond minimal survival) will contaminate the sincerity of their intent or devalue their talent in some way, or even unspiritualise (yeah, thought the dictionary would hate that one ...) them in some way.

So these, in many cases, most admirable of folk remain in Struggle and even perpetuate the struggle and are always on some or other detour away from wealth, because that way they keep their Specialness intact. They refuse to embrace life and simply flow – for if they did and if they embraced wealth they would become like everyone else – no longer very special.

This of course is another huge misconception – because, let's face it, what would we do and where would the world be without the saviours, anarchists, do-gooders? Where would we be without people willing to risk life and limb in service of others? How awesome is it to do this, and what homage should we be paying to those who so serve? They are indeed special and this Specialness should be especially rewarded.

As should be those who hold the space for our spirit to expand – through beautiful art, music, literature, dance. What homage should we be paying to such offerings?

And how we should be ensuring that those who help to uplift anyone and anything in any way should be massively rewarded!

But, meanwhile, until the mass consensus thinking comes to the party (which one, does not matter at the moment), I would like each and every one of the people on the Specialness detour to take the blinkers off and get back on track! To do and to continue doing your great tasks and missions requires much cash – you need to stop struggling and allow the great wall of money that is headed your way to flow. Then, you can direct it towards wondrous upliftment, beauty, and fabulous deeds.

Begin now to acknowledge, believe, assert, and spread the fact that the money needs to be in *your* hands. For if you really believed that money would be better off used for the higher good in your butterfly-saving project than in the design of some killer stilettos, then you have to make that known in the world. First you have to believe that, if you really believe it (if you know what I mean). You have to reach out and take that money and use it to build those homes. You have to trust that what you do is special, valuable, worthy of money – large, vast, huge sums of money. For if you don't believe it, who will?

There is also another category of Specialness I would like to cover. This is the Specialness of the intellectual. Some writers (especially those of *really* good literature) fall into this category too, as do other intellectual types: inventors, mathematicians, professors, anthropologists and the like. These special folk do a reverse sort of snobbery. Like, 'We are way too clever to go for something as dumb and ordinary and mediocre as money', 'Only dumb, ordinary, mediocre people chase money. We chase wonderful theorems and structures of reality that prove that the monetary system does not exist' ... or that it is a fascist plot and so on. 'We are way too intelligent to follow cash.' It's a shame and a waste of some good minds, this sort of Specialness. These folk are always on a detour to create a new barter system or to debunk solar power in favour of wind.

End the struggle. Get back on track. The world needs you!!

A light task:	Discover what you could do to uplift the world if money flowed.
	Reflect on how you are the same as everyone else.
	Reflect on how you are special.
Inspired Action:	*Seek and find money where you would not normally look*

Park your ego: Focus your intent to serve
Get back on track

Commitment: I dedicate myself to special deeds which warrant great reward

Everyone is special: no one is special
The only thing that is special is our deeds

4. Fourth Wealth Detour – GREED
– *Chasing what you don't have*
– Grow the half-full glass

Now we all want to skip this chapter. We all think greed is something that does not apply to us. Have you ever met anyone who said, 'Yes, I remember a time when I was greedy'? Or, 'I am a really greedy so-and-so, especially when it comes to paying out bonuses'. I very much doubt it.

Everyone believes greed is something that happens to some other person out there. We all know what he looks like, don't we? He's old, male, scrawny, with beard or stubble, dressed in a frayed collar and worn shoes. He lives in an old house packed high with every issue of the morning newspaper since 1953, and he lives on tinned tomato soup and crackers.

However, greed is the emotion that most consumerist marketing hopes to evoke when they tantalise us with things we do not have – never mind if we need them. Greed is a great detour on the road to wealth. It takes us off our purpose. It dilutes our intent. Greed is the road to pursuing what we don't have, instead of the road to what we do. Now this may sound both obvious and in some sense crazy, but I will explain.

Greed is not only when we look at the half full glass and see it as half empty, but it's also when we then focus on the half empty to such an extent that it spreads – because what we focus on expands – filling the whole glass with emptiness.

When we focus on what we have and how to grow that, how to make more of that, it is very different from focusing on what we don't have and wishing it was different, or wondering why the 'don't have' is there, or growing the 'don't have' into a bigger 'don't have'.

This takes many forms, some very subtle, all of which amount to greed. I will give you some examples. I remember a company who was paying commission for business signed, taking the decision to reduce their commission structure, when some of the sales people started earning very large sums of money.

The focus of the people who took this decision was clearly and quite erroneously in the wrong place. Instead of looking at what they had, i.e. more business coming in, and seeing if perhaps they could increase this further by rewarding the high production of those sales people by offering even greater incentives, they were instead focusing on (the little) they didn't have, i.e. what they were paying out in commission. They wanted that too. Pure greed.

What happens in such a case is that you detour off the wealth path on a path of chasing what you don't have and the end result of that is that you always land up with even less. It's obvious to see how this will happen in the above example.

To have more you need to contain more

Another example. You've been selling shoes on terms and this is how you've always operated. You have some regular buyers who have always supported you. They spread the word about your shoes and more and more people buy them. Now your shoes are in great demand and some of the new buyers enquire about buying large quantities. You decide that anyone wanting your shoes in future must pay a deposit, and you start by asking for one from your existing clients. Your sales decrease.

What both these examples have in common is the inability to contain. And indeed to have more you need to contain more. Greed is a detour which dissipates containment. Greed is an attempt to contain more which is ineffectively executed because instead of trying to contain, one is trying to 'get' more. More is coming in, but one is not seeing it. One is not focusing on containing what is already there and growing that. One is looking to see where or how one could be losing. This is a big mistake and a huge detour.

To determine whether one of your plans to expand or 'improve your system of operation' in the face of expansion, real or looming, is motivated by greed, ask yourself the following questions:

- Is this idea motivated by a fear of loss? For example, 'Look how much commission we are losing when these sales people keep bringing in all this new business'; or 'What if all these new clients don't pay – let's get a deposit'.
- Does my plan reward expansion or growth or new business?
- Does my plan arise from a desire to contain (and grow) the half full glass, or to protect against the half empty glass growing? And, no, it cannot do both! Period.

Although the Greed detour can occur at any point along the Wealth Consciousness scale, it does correlate with the Wealth Consciousness of Dependence and the wealth challenge of Control – Expand.

The answer is to clarify focus through cultivating generosity and openness. When more is coming in you need to celebrate, give more, open, thereby focusing on what you have, rather than what you don't have. This is an act of expansion, whereas Greed contracts.

A light task:	Discover which part of the half full, half empty glass you focus on. Reflect on where your life and wealth are full. Reflect on how you can expand that which is full.
Inspired Action:	*Reward expansion* *Replace acts of Greed with acts of containment* *Get back on track*

Commitment: As I expand so I focus on what I have and on its containment

5. Fifth Wealth Detour – COMPLICATION – *Losing the plot* – Simplify your life

It's very easy to become confused in this world. It's very easy to lose focus, and purpose. It is indeed far easier for a camel to pass through the eye of a needle these days than it is to remain on track with your wealth programme. And that's because we have overcomplicated life to such an extent that the simplest thing has become a full-on production – while, at the same time, we have actually convinced ourselves that this full-on production is making our lives easier, simpler and faster.

Witness the ease and speed with which one previously set a date (way back in the dark ages before technology).

Ring, Ring (the telephone – just a plain ring – no erotic giggling, cat meowing or disco music).

'Hi, how are you doing?'

'Great, how about you?'

'I'm fine. I was wondering if you want to meet for a spot of tea? Say at Mamaduke's?'

'That sounds good. What time?'

'3pm?'

'No, I have tennis, what about four?'

'Four's no good but I can do 4.30.'

'That's great! See you then.'

Speak this out loud and time it. Then, do it on a mobile, back and forth, even with letters replacing words. In any language. Time that. C? I mean?

You want to write down an appointment in your diary? Well, I can tell you I have whipped out my teensy little book (made from real paper) and opened it up and picked a date and am busy writing (with a real ink pen) while the speedy mobile is still finding the diary entries. Fact.

Our world has become very complicated, even as we believe that it is simpler, easier, faster than it was before. It's generally not. Generally we have more to do each day. Emails to check, delete, file, respond to, get back to to read on another day, forward, unsubscribe from. Text messages to ditto. Facebook to update on what's happening in our lives, what we just read, what movies our friends watched recently. Then Twitter for that minute-by-minute monitoring of who has a sale and where we had our cappuccino this morning. Too much information. Too much distraction. Too much confusion. Too much complication.

The average person has become so lost and confused that they now need a bevy of consultants, coaches, analysts and therapists to tell them what to do. The real reason that coaching is the fastest growing profession in the world at the moment, in my opinion, is that everyone is totally and severely overstimulated, dazed and confused, stressed and not coping.

We work harder and harder so we can earn more and more so we can have more and more (and more) gadgets and things and programmes and groups so that our lives can become more and more (and more) full and complicated, so we can have less and less and less time, so we can be more and more (and more) confused, distracted, overworked, and stressed – by all this information and all the gadgets which we think are making our lives easier and simpler.

WAKE UP! Technology was supposed to give us more leisure time. By now, in the fabulous year so way beyond 2000, we were supposed to be working three-day weeks and having four-day weekends – at the very least. What happened to that?

Okay, back to wealth detours. So many people lose their way on the Wealth Journey because they become confused. The handling of money itself can become totally wrapped in confusion once you connect with 'clever' accounting and begin to borrow and gear and wriggle and wangle your way through each month. Soon, very soon, you have lost the plot.

We are both the creators and the travellers of all our journeys

You have forgotten that all you wanted was to pay off your house and have more time with the children, and do some gardening. Now, you have three houses, three gardeners, three maids, a housekeeper and a cook, you have to work weekends, you never see the children who are taken from one activity to the next by the au pair, who also accompanies you on holiday (in case you have to zip back to the office at short notice – which is more often than not the case). But you remind yourself of the great and wonderful opportunities your children have (which you did not have), and console your guilty conscience with the purchase of another car or i-pod. Sound familiar?

End the struggle. End the confusion. Get back your focus. Get back on track. Become wealthy. Find out what that means. Today already!

Do you still remember what you want? Do you know what you need? How much of what you're trying to acquire, achieve, finance, create, is really what you really, really want? When exactly are you going to pursue what you really, really want? How about today?

Get back on track!

Complication creates confusion. The best way to cut through confusion is to prioritise. When you prioritise, look at what's important, not what's urgent. Look at what would make you happy. Look at what would enhance your life.

Remember that 20% of our actions/energy/focus creates 80% of our results. Really reflect on this with a view to eliminating the 80% unnecessary action/energy/focus.

Confusion takes many forms. And as everything is connected, confusion in one area of life will reflect in confusion in another. Confusion can also mean entanglement. When your fingers are in too many pies, nothing is ever quite finished, you're running from place to place putting out fires, you don't know what's going on. When this happens you are definitely off track.

You need to disentangle your affairs. Prioritise. Finish things off. Deliver. Complete. End the confusion through exercising choice. Decide what you want. Decide what you are doing. Decide where you are going. Get back on track.

A light task:	Discover what it is that wealth means to you.
	Reflect on what would add value to your life.
Inspired Action:	*Simplify! Simplify! Simplify!*
	Remove the 80% unnecessary action
	Get back on track

Commitment: I focus only on what adds value to my life

6. Sixth Wealth Detour – AMBIGUITY
– *Trying to walk two roads at once*
– Commit to what you want

Ambiguity is similar to confusion, but also very different. Ambiguity is when you stop moving along your wealth path, or when you come to a crossroads and keep running down one path and back and then down the other path and back; or when you reach a circle and keep going round and round variously trying different paths that lead off the centre. You are not on any path because you are trying to cover too many bases.

When you do this your energy and focus become dispersed. In real life it's when what you really want is to become a film director, but you are actually running a production company, while freelancing as an assistant director for extra cash. The real problem though is that you believe producing is not creative and being an assistant director is something beneath you, while doubting you can get the financing for the direction of your movie. Very little will happen here until you make a stand – and this is based on a real life case scenario.

You cannot walk all these paths simultaneously. Sure, you may be looking at increasing your wealth profile, but this will be an exceedingly hard way to do it. What this scenario lacks is commitment. And the mental and energetic commitment is what comes first. That is what drives the physical, bringing what you want into being.

Making a commitment ends ambiguity and puts you back on track. You cannot sit on the fence, or cover all your bases and expect to make progress along your wealth path, because quite simply you cannot travel two or three or in any case any more than one path at a time. Forget multitasking.

I recently read in the *Financial Times* that (most disappointingly for the researchers who were hoping for a different outcome), according to the latest research, people who (apparently) multitask, neither complete things, nor do things well, and nor do they actually multitask at all. This of course throws a bit of a spanner in the 'observer affects the observed' theory too – but perhaps the researchers were not close enough to their subjects, or maybe their manifestation skills were under par. In any event, the researchers were hoping to discover some sort of superior gene or aptitude possessed by multitaskers but, alas, on the contrary, it was very much a case of Jack of all trades but master of none – literally.

The fact is the mind can only focus on one thing at a time – that's it, really. And so when it comes to focusing on creating an outcome – like, say, wealth, you need to be clear – in fact, crystal clear. You need to know what you want quite specifically, and then focus your attention, intention, activities, actions, energy, and focus (yes indeed, focus your focus) on that thing. In other words, stay on track. The minute you start with the 'what ifs', you're at that roundabout and taking a detour.

This can happen anywhere along the Wealth Journey. In terms of the Wealth Consciousness levels it correlates with Independence and deciding what to do with it – often we try to 'diversify' before we've become firmly and fully grounded. Just as money starts to come in we rush off on not one, not two, but three (often hare-brained) new money-making schemes/ investments/expansions – in other words, diversions.

Stick to the path. This is the time to clarify your purpose – clearly. (Yes indeed, we have focusing your focus and clarifying clearly!) Purpose is a longer-term picture than survival. Where are you going? What are you doing? What do you want?

We are definitely looking at the wealth challenge of Dissipate : Contain. This is the detour that may lead from that challenge if it's not properly integrated. We need to contain. And to do that we need a specific container, goal, destination – the subject of *The Money Well*™ book.

Ambiguity is not the result of not knowing what you want – it's the result of not committing to the thing you know you want because you are too afraid to commit. And you don't want to commit because you are afraid both to achieve it, and also not to achieve it. You don't want to stick your neck out. So you hedge your bets. Hedging sucks! It's wimpish and it's beige and just don't do it. (Unless you are a hedge trader, that is ...)

Now, having a strategy is not the same as not committing. For example, many, many moons ago I was telemarketing on straight commission with a view to earning what I wanted while working half day. For the first eight months I did not earn, which necessitated my getting an evening sales job to earn some cash to keep me going. But this evening job was never a deviation from my course. I did not doubt my day job, or what I could achieve there. I did not take the night job 'in case the day one did not work out'. My attention and focus and intent continued to be on my day job – which worked so well that eventually I owned that company. And just as soon as I started earning in my day job, I dropped the night one like a hot cake.

Having a strategy is not a detour if you remain focused and keep your intent intact. Ambiguity starts and grows first in the mind. Be clear about what you want and where you are going.

We are the light that illuminates our path

I know people who, while consulting for companies on a monthly rate, are simultaneously running several other businesses none of which are particularly excelling. Also, the net effect of all this activity is not affluence, but rather extreme stress and debt. However, they are loath to stop, to unplug their energy, attention, and focus from some of these ventures and to rather channel their efforts in one direction. Although there would no doubt be an initial short-term decrease in earnings, the long-term effect would be enormously positive. The immediate effect on energy levels would be huge! The clarity of mind that would result, enabling proper focus and direction of intent, would be immeasurable.

I was once told by Rob Nairn, author of *Tranquil Mind*, that it is better to take twelve steps along one path than two steps each along six different paths. I often think of his words.

So commit. Focus. Get back on track. Stay on one path.

A light task: Reflect on where your energy and focus dissipate.

Discover what path you should be on

Inspired Action: *Gather your energy, attention, focus, and intent*
Remove distraction
Get back on track

Commitment: I commit to getting what I want

7. Seventh Wealth Detour – PROCRASTINATION
– *The thief of wealth*
– Take the next step

Procrastination comes in many forms – and is not as obvious as we imagine. The main reason for procrastination is doubt. We put off doing things because we are in doubt about something – usually our intuition or thinking. Though it's true that we sometimes need to get more information on which to base a decision, generally we simply do not trust ourselves. We fear getting it wrong, so we procrastinate. This procrastination can cost us lots of opportunity. It may waste huge resources as we try to do market research, or create reports or investigate what we want to do before we start doing it. We delay, looking for confirmation, afraid to make a mistake. We consult tarot readers, or fortune-tellers or our horoscopes. Or we may even see a professional and try to get them to make the decision for us.

We make starting or continuing with our wealth creation plan dependent on something else. It's a bit of a variation on Excuses. We say, when this happens or that happens, *then* I can do it. We delay our Wealth Journey or the expansion of our wealth because we cannot accommodate, embrace, have, or contain more.

It's easy to procrastinate on the Wealth Consciousness level of Comfort as there is no pressing need to do anything, things are ticking by. In fact many people become stuck in Comfort for that very reason.

Often we avoid taking a step that would lead us to the next level on our Wealth Journey because we fear change. Because energy needs to keep moving, it is not possible merely to stop, so our procrastination usually results in performing at a tangent. We try to keep or be or become busy doing something that actually has nothing to do with what we are doing, but we convince ourselves that we are still working towards our goal.

The greatest procrastination manoeuvres usually occur at points of great transition – when we are on the brink of taking the next big step. That's when we discover we absolutely have to have a new accounting system. Or we cannot continue without new offices or we refuse to look at our profitability or to address staff who are costing us money or to confront some other unpleasantness that needs to be changed in order to get to the next level until the new computer system is up and running.

Procrastination takes enormous energy. It's a detour that can keep us permanently off course, because with procrastination we get so involved doing other things we lose the way to our goal. We may even forget where we were going in the first place. We get caught up in fixing things which becomes crisis management, and because this seems to be so noble and important and meaningful, we begin to believe that *this* is what we are meant to be doing – we lose our way.

Procrastination is the act of putting focus on the things that are not important. We delay doing the important stuff till last. We avoid success and wealth. We put it off and put it off until eventually it goes away.

Don't delay! Get wealthy today!

*A **light task:***	Reflect on how you procrastinate. List those things and activities which you most avoid.
Inspired Action:	*Commit to getting important things done first* *Stop delay* *Do the things that create wealth*

Commitment: I do what creates or enhances wealth

8. Eighth Wealth Detour – ILLUSION
– *Starting from where you're not*
– Be Here. Be Now. Be You

Eight is the number of abundance, and wealth expansion, and the eighth wealth detour deals with Illusion, which is very fitting. This is one of the most powerful detours in terms of how much energy will become available once this detour is properly channelled, and redirected towards one's goal.

Illusion is a terrible detour as it keeps you totally misinformed and misdirected while you continue to think you are on course. The problem with illusion is just that – it's an illusion. It is not the truth. It is not the way things are. And while you are looking at what is not, you cannot change it. While you do not start from where you are, you can get nowhere. You can change something only when you know what it is. You can begin a journey only from where you are right now.

The detour of Illusion keeps you going from nowhere to

nowhere, forever chasing something from where you're not. How can you be where you're not? I will give you an example.

A really dear lady in my practice is unencumbered, without debt, without commitments, without fixed assets like a home, but with a considerable sum in liquid cash from which she maintains what is a modest but would be for many an enviable living. She is a free agent who spends her days pursuing her hobbies, socialising, travelling and expanding her knowledge of self.

Although she is a woman of a 'certain' age, she is fit, healthy and attractive. All in all – and in fact in every way, she is to be envied. However, she has spent many years demeaning herself, her wealth and what she considers to be her 'bad management' of this money. She has many historical regrets – wishing she had invested in a home or in some other asset which could have appreciated more meaningfully than cash.

When she first started to see me, her conversation revolved around what she could not have with her money. How she could not have the house she wanted, how the money she had was all the money she had in the world, how once it was finished, it would no longer be there, how what she needed was more money and how 'stupid' her decision making, her money management and her life management were too.

So this dear lady viewed the world in terms of what the money she had did not give her – trying to get to the place of owning a house she could not afford; trying to get to a place where she had more money (for the house she could not afford). She wanted to not be the person who has what she has. She wanted to be someone who historically had made other decisions.

And in doing the above, she was not embracing and containing what she has. She was not starting where she is.

She was trying to go somewhere from where she's not. In other words, she was not in the present.

And looking at the present for a moment, we have a healthy, attractive, unencumbered woman with a positive cash balance who can go anywhere from 'HERE'. And as 'a healthy, attractive, unencumbered woman with a positive cash balance' she would be going somewhere quite different from where 'a "stupid" woman with no business sense, no assets and no home who is about to run out of all the money she has in the world' would be going. Either way, she can never get from 'where I would have been if I had made better decisions' to 'the house I can't afford to buy', as both are illusions.

The good news is that even as I write this, she is reconfiguring her beliefs and viewpoint, connecting with the present and practising looking at what is: i.e. that she is an awesome woman in an enviable position! And I have no doubt that before I finish this book, she will be manifesting something truly fabulous in her life!

But let's get back to Illusion. Most of us live there, most of the time. Another lady I saw recently, discovered that after two decades in a marriage, she had been living with a picture of that marriage which existed only in her head. The reality of the situation was that the relationship had never really worked. Not only that, but she had never even really loved the man in the first place! Quite a thing to discover twenty years down the line – but better than discovering it after forty!

Illusion in the arena of money works in many ways. All of them relate to *trying to get somewhere from where you're not*. And sometimes trying to get to 'who knows where' or to 'where you could have been' or to 'where you can't get at this very moment' from 'where you're not, but wished you had been'. It's really a waste of time and energy to do this.

You cannot get to 'where you're going' from 'where you're not'

'Where you're not' is a state of denial of both the positive (as in the case of the first dear lady) and the negative as in the case of the many people in the world who are seriously and over their heads in debt, and in some cases even bankrupt, but continue to live *'la vida loca'* believing that they are in fact well off.

You get on the Illusion detour (metaphorically – for those who are literal ...) by shutting your eyes, or becoming disorientated in some way – like you stand on your head and suddenly everything seems upside down – but it's just you, standing on your head. Or you start to think the road is a river, or the sun blinds you and everything seems to have a halo around it, and you pursue the halo. You are just not seeing reality as it is.

When this happens it's good to take some impartial, outside input – let someone else (who has no vested interest, and definitely not a partner or lover or spouse) tell you what they see.

A good starting point is to count your blessings. Look at what is happening in your life which is good. Look at what's working. Look at what you can build on. Also look at what's not working. What needs to change or transform. When you look, look at what is. And what is, is always in the present. Come into the present. That's the only place from which you can move forward.

A light task: Reflect on where you are.
Count your blessings.
Find those things in your life that
you can rejoice about.

Inspired Action: *Commit to doing things that are in the present*
See someone who can add perspective

Commitment: I move forward from where I am

9. Ninth Wealth Detour – FEAR
– Not taking up your power
– Serve

Now it may seem that Fear should be one of the first detours to deal with rather than the last. Fear is certainly a detour that appears all along the Wealth Journey. It leads us up a dead-end street from which there is often no return. But the most poignant place for Fear to create a detour is when we have arrived at Wealth, or Affluence.

Fear takes many forms and expresses itself in a variety of detours. Always, fear is the detour we take when we try to get away from something that hasn't yet happened. We fear it *may* happen. And when we catch wind of even the possibility of it happening, we bolt down the nearest detour.

Fear is another form of Illusion. It is a place of 'not being' that we hope not to go to. But we can never get to 'not there', and certainly not from 'not here'. So what happens (because everything is connected) is that the 'not there' that we project starts to affect the 'here and now', distorting it into a place from where the 'not there' can happen.

Let me explain that another way. A chair can only cast the shadow of a chair. But as everything is conscious and everything is energy, and everything is connected, if the chair started to view its shadow as a mug often enough, and if it feared its shadow becoming a mug strongly enough, then with time, not only would the shadow start transforming into a mug, but the chair itself would become a mug too. Okay, so maybe that's a little out there as an example for many – but it certainly will leave a clear image in your mind to work with.

What I'm saying is that what you focus on expands. And fear closes doors and possibilities. Fear shrinks reality. In fact fear distorts reality into the very thing you are trying to avoid. Fear is a big, fat magnifying glass.

And what are we afraid of? We fear success. We fear failure. We fear not being accepted for who we are. We fear change. We fear changing. In fact we fear fear itself. This feels very déjà vu – I think I may have said these very words somewhere in this book before.

Mostly, we fear coming into our power. Owning up to it. Taking responsibility. Becoming more of who we are. Flying. And this is why I have put fear last and am in a sense aligning it with the Wealth Consciousness level of Affluence, and the wealth challenge of Power.

Fear anywhere shrinks you, but Fear at Affluence or Wealth shrinks the planet.

Fear begins in the mind. It is projected from the mind, creating a thought form which many others join into, onto, and with, resulting in the creation of the many things we do not want on this planet.

The responsibility of those in Wealth or Affluence is to properly align their thinking so that it benefits all. The responsibility of those with power is to use that power to benefit as many people as possible. Fear stops all that.

When you take the wealth detour of Fear your actions become diminished. It's like arriving at the well of plenty and trying to reverse its flow and shrink it back into the pipe it flowed through once, which is somehow linked to you. The pipe is too small. The well is now bigger than you and the pipe. If you try to force the flow backwards the pipe will burst. Also, if you try to keep the well to yourself, maintain it so nothing is lost, it will stagnate and sour.

When you have detoured due to fear you can feel it. Firstly, your sense of possibilities seems lost. Suddenly dead-ends surround you. The future begins to look bleak. You suspect that the business that you have spent so many years bringing to this point, may not be the business you want to be in after all. You suddenly feel 'scaling down' in some way is what is called for in your life. You start to wonder what it's all about and whether there is a deeper meaning to life, to your purpose.

These are all very good and very definite calls to service, to the need to take up your power and wield it for the greater good. It is time to expand. All you need to do when you're in a cul-de-sac is to turn around – then suddenly, the road is clear. Turning around is a decision and a choice. The choice is determined by your intent. Ask yourself:

How can I serve the greater whole?

A light task:	Reflect on coming into your power. What could you do to serve, today?
Inspired Action:	*Commit to service*
	Commit to serving the greater whole
	Connect with Spirit

Commitment: I flow and grow towards the greater good for all

We have come to the end of the wealth detours! Phew!

The key thing to remember with a detour is to get back on track. Don't sit down a deep dark hole, or in a thicket or in a cul-de-sac trying to figure out how you got there, or why you're there. Change your mind. Change your story. Change your viewpoint. Get back on track. Recognise where you are, express the desire to change, commit your will and intent to the change, make the change and get back on track.

6

What To Do Once You Get There

Living the 9 I's of wealth

1. I am here – Reality check
2. I acknowledge the way I feel – Decompression
3. I pay attention – Focus
4. I am content – Containment
5. I am at the destination I have chosen – Fine-tuning
6. I rejoice – Celebrate!
7. I expand – New space
8. I dream – New reality
9. I am wealthy – Be

Living the 9 I's of wealth is an exercise in opening one's eyes (sorry, couldn't resist that!). It is the process of coming into the present and aligning with where you are. Living the 9 I's has to be done at every step along the Wealth Consciousness ladder in order to successfully integrate and move on to the next step.

Because we live in such a fast paced and complicated world we do not take the time to reflect and to integrate. No sooner have we arrived somewhere than we are off again, at speed. Even before we've actually landed, we are busy moving to the next place.

The commercials tell us this is a mighty fine thing to do. We are shown people gobbling down food, turning green with indigestion, and then after popping a pill or drinking some medicine, they can continue drinking and eating more(!?). We see stressed, harassed mothers rushing from place to place being 'too busy to get a headache' so they take a pill and continue to rush into the night. This is considered to be a good thing in our world.

Most of the planet suffers from indigestion – mental, physical, emotional and spiritual. On the Wealth Journey, many people get so caught up in accumulating and rushing and working, they never integrate their gains. And when the consciousness of wealth is not integrated, one never becomes truly wealthy – no matter how much is in the bank. Not only that, but one is never happy either. There is no contentment. No sense of taking credit. And as a result, a vicious cycle is set up where because the wealth is not integrated, it is not contained, therefore it dissipates and the cycle of accumulation and of needing and wanting starts all over again.

Living the 9 I's of wealth is like a training manual for containment. Where *Money Well*™ looked at 'How to contain wealth', here we will look at a step-by-step process of ensuring continued containment and contentment.

For what is the point of going through a journey, unless we also enjoy arriving at the destination? And beyond that we need to know what to do once we've arrived. That is what this section is all about.

1. First I – I am here – Reality check

The first thing to do when you arrive is to recognise that your journey is at an end. You have arrived!

We usually arrive panting, exhausted, stressed and sometimes even burnt out. We are so wound up that we need time to unravel. We have so struggled and stressed to get here that part of us does not even realise we are here at all. Our minds are still back 'there'. Our pattern of striving is so firmly entrenched that even when we try to stop, our mind continues to race around on its hamster wheel, computing, planning, angst-ing. Part of us does not believe we have arrived at all. We need to catch up and get our bearings.

In my previous books I tell the story of how I set a goal of becoming financially independent from humble beginnings, how I achieved that goal, and how I then went on to write and teach about wealth creation. But that is only half of the story, or maybe two thirds. The other third is the story of what happened between my arriving at my financially independent situation (full of assets, a beach house, fancy cars, no debt, and even a wonderful new man) and my writing and teaching.

That has been a whole journey in itself and one which I have been aware needs telling. And it occurs to me now, a decade after that point of my 'arriving' that I would not have had a section called 'Living the 9 I's of wealth – what to do when you get there' had I not had the experiences that I did.

I, probably like many others before me, thought that all I had to do when my goal was achieved was to arrive. But arriving, properly arriving, is something that took me many, many years to do. And it definitely ties in with the finishing part of a cycle which we covered before – the fact that when you finish, you must finish properly, in order to end a cycle.

When I arrived I was stressed, burnt-out and anxious. I was suffering post-traumatic stress disorder after an armed hijacking experience I had coolly handled and walked from a good twelve months before. At the time of the incident, I had simply carried on with life – too busy to let fear get in the way.

I was exhausted from so much – holding the energy for the sale of my business to go through for many months, concluding the sale itself. I had worked day and night for years. I was also processing grief I'd had no time to deal with – my mother had passed away in the middle of negotiations, and I'd left everything and everyone I knew behind when I moved to Cape Town.

You have not arrived until you really get here

So let's say when I 'arrived' I had baggage, lots of baggage. And just because the reality around me was fantastic, this did not mean my baggage had miraculously disappeared. And we will deal with baggage in the next section.

The thing to do when you arrive is to get your bearings. Simply look at where you are. Acknowledge what is. Say 'Here I am in a beautiful space – I have arrived at my destination. I have everything to be grateful for. I have every reason to celebrate. But I am sad. I feel lost. I feel bereft. I feel stressed out. And I have baggage. So I need time.' I didn't do this, so it took so much longer.

Simply accepting where you are and how you are feeling is a way of coming into the present. Unfortunately, if we are tired and exhausted, as I was, we spend much time pretending to be happy or berating ourselves for not being as joyful as the situation demands.

In a sense, the first thing to do when you arrive is to STOP. Get off the plane, or the bus or the yak. Look around.

On Wealth Arrival – Reality check:

- Where are you?
- Do you have all your luggage?
- What baggage do you have?
- How do you feel?
- What are you missing?

These questions can be answered on many levels. The main thing to realise is that *that journey is over*.

Realisation: *That journey is over. I have arrived at a new place*

Focus: Take time and space to rest

There is always a sense of loss at the end of any journey – even if the journey was bumpy as hell. That bears recognising too. At the first 'I' you need to simply acknowledge where you are. Take stock. Then rest. Take time and space to be. The length of this can vary. I know people who have taken a year to unravel after the sale of their business. If you are between levels of Wealth Consciousness it may be simply a few hours or a day or long weekend you need for this step. The key is to stop when you arrive and to simply acknowledge the fact.

2. Second I – I acknowledge the way I feel – Decompression

A lot of the baggage we bring to our destination is nothing more than compressed time. That is, emotions, tiredness, stress, thinking, that we never allowed enough time to experience, unfold, process or unravel.

It's like missing a few nights' sleep. You need to catch up. When we arrive at our wealth destination, depending on how old we are, and how fast or hard we have lived, we may have more than the equivalent of one or two nights to catch up on – of sleep, of rest, of stress release, of just pure being.

First we need to recognise that we have baggage. That it did not just vanish because we have arrived. We need to acknowledge that we have not changed from the day before we received twelve million pounds to the day after. Our bank balance has changed. Our work scenario may have changed – in fact we may no longer have 'work' per se – and this is an anxiety producing feeling in itself for most. We are no longer needed. And if you've spent your life working, arriving at an office each day, planning and doing, the thought of suddenly 'doing nothing' – though you may have fantasised over that very possibility for decades – is, in actual reality, exceedingly scary.

Which brings us to another aspect of baggage – the new feelings that our affluent situation evokes. Because many of these feelings – fear, insecurity, anxiety – are so similar to the old feelings of lack which we were trying to transcend on our journey to wealth, that the two types of baggage become mingled and confused. Also, because these feelings are so at odds with what the physical reality of our situation seems to demand (we are rich, for heaven's sake!), we try to refuse acknowledging that we are feeling them.

So here we are – wealthy, successful, having arrived at our goal, our longed for destination and we may, after the initial adrenalin rush of hurrah, hurrah, has worn off, feel pretty devastated.

Apart from the reasons I mentioned before – historical compression of stress and emotions, and present time anxiety and stress over what is a rather radical change in life and status – the other reason these emotions arise and emerge, is simply because you now have time to deal with them.

We are extremely intelligent and efficient organisms. Our bodies are very wise and effective. So at the first opportunity for healing and release, our systems are full steam ahead!

In my case, I really fell apart both emotionally and physically. Physically I had been very fit and healthy, supple and trim, exercising four to five times a week, eating healthily (when I had time to eat), mostly vegetarian, but with a history of migraine type headaches which I had chosen to override and medicate to keep going during my years in business.

Unwind, unwind, unwind

When I 'arrived' I was planning to upgrade my fitness levels (naturally ...) – engage my own t'ai-chi master for daily sessions, go hiking, get a tan. But within a few months, I was totally, and literally, incapacitated. I slipped and fell and my lower back and neck (which I was later told had been needing attention for a decade and a half) went into a six-year process of healing. Not only could I not exercise – and, believe me, I tried each and every type of exercise possible – I could hardly walk. I was in almost constant pain. I was releasing pain.

I also had to release fear and anxiety. I slept a lot. I was very tired, even though I was doing very little. I was also confused and stressed, mostly because I did not think I should be feeling this way. I did not think I should be falling apart. I did not think my body should be packing up on me now.

I remember many of my clients from the fund management days having very similar experiences on their retirement. Many became ill and depressed after their businesses were sold. Others felt anxious about the future and did not know what to do with their days.

It is good to know that this is normal. It is (or may be) one of the phases and stages of arriving at wealth. It is good to take the time to take stock of baggage, unfinished business if you like. Be aware that there are emotions, stress, possibly even physical conditions that may need decompression and unravelling. On the other hand, if you are feeling just absolutely great – WELL DONE! You can skip this section!

Reflect on your journey to this place of wealth. Reflect on what needs to decompress.

On Wealth Arrival – Decompress:

- What emotions need to decompress?
- What have you been putting a lid on?
- What baggage did you bring from your journey?
- How does your body feel? How do you feel?
- What do you need to unwind and unravel?

These questions can be answered on many levels. The main thing to realise is that *you may have baggage from your journey.* But if you don't – don't create stress over that ...

Realisation: *I need time to unwind myself*

Focus: Get help to unravel – body work, mind work, meditation, rest

Many people die as a result of lack of decompression. They hold on to unexpressed emotions, old conditions, loads of stress. Take the time to catch up. Wealth is the place to unravel.

3. Third I – I pay attention – Focus

Once you have stopped, seen where you are and decompressed, it's time to pay attention. In other words you need to look around, because in a sense the first two I's were like a transition period. Now, you have to pay attention to what is happening as well as to what you may be ignoring.

Of course the second bit may not be as easy as it seems, but it is in fact a lot easier than it sounds. Usually we ignore, and miss and overlook *the obvious*. For instance, as I point out often, both in my books and in my sessions and courses, profit is the first thing to focus on when you are in business. When I mention that, most people dismiss the notion with a hand wave saying something like 'of course, that goes without saying'. But when I highlight how they may not in fact have as much as mentioned it in any way, directly or indirectly; and when I ask them to consider if profit is what they focus their intent on, they begin to see the light. And then ... (and this is the really wonderful part) when the light goes on and they realign themselves and their employees and their business to put profit up there as their intent ... then wealth suddenly pours in.

When you arrive at you destination of wealth there is much to pay attention to. A lot of obvious stuff is overlooked, often because it's so obvious, and sometimes because we become so overwhelmed. For a start, we need to look at our money, and with a view to containing it and protecting it from leaking. We must pay attention to our health – especially if we begin to unravel per the previous section. We must ensure loved ones continue to be taken care of if we are falling apart. In other words, somehow, we need to make sure that things do not fall apart around us while we are in transition, trying to catch up with and absorb our new situation.

In essence we are in no-man's-land – a space between time and place. We are at the end of one thing and just before the beginning of another. Nothing exists here, and we need to ensure we do not become stuck or lost. We must keep one eye on the past and the other on the future. Time indeed does seem suddenly to lose meaning, and it may whizz past so that you are left unable to account for what you've been doing for the last eight or eighteen months or it may drag on and on through each hour.

The important thing is to somehow pay attention and not lose sight of where you are (at the end of a journey, and at wealth), what you are doing (taking a breather and orientating), and where you are going (to become a writer and teacher in my case). So do not become distracted – going back into a business unrelated to your quest, as I did.

What you focus on expands

Do not forget to pay your bills and water your plants either. In fact it may be a good thing if you are taking a breather to pay all your running costs for a year in advance (you can afford it, after all) so you have less to worry about.

As for your money, it needs attention too. You need to look

at what you will be doing with it, and although the urge to spend, spend, spend will be there, I suggest you put (the bulk of) your money somewhere where you can't touch it for a year. That's after you settle all and any debt in full. Try to avoid long-term commitments while you are in this in-between space. Avoid any clever and especially get-rich-quick schemes, and approach the once-in-a-lifetime-opportunities with extreme caution. I would suggest avoiding them all together, until you have properly landed, got your bearings, and found out what you are doing and where you're going.

On Wealth Arrival – Pay Attention:

- What do I need to notice?
- What am I not paying attention to or seeing?
- What is obvious?
- How can I protect my wealth?
- What debt can I clear?

These questions can be answered on many levels. The main thing to realise is that *you must pay attention to your life and wealth.*

Realisation: *I need to look at the obvious*

Focus: Contain, watch, remain vigilant

4. Fourth I – I am content – Containment

The fourth I, and one of the most important aspects of the entire Wealth Journey, is contentment and containment. The reason we get financial indigestion (which results in our having to void our metaphorical financial stomach) is that we do not take the time to contain and be content. The next three levels may all be happening at once – containing, rejoicing and fine-tuning, but I will deal with them individually.

Once you are over the shock and trauma of your arrival, once you've got your bearings, once you're quite clear on the fact that you have arrived, you need to contain and be content. Count your blessings! Be grateful! Sit back, take a deep sigh and relax.

Being content is a fine skill to cultivate. Being content is the realisation that everything is as it should be. Contentment is recognition – of a job well done, of a goal achieved, of life flowing, of health, of wealth, of having enough, of divine relationships and friendships, of the magnificence of a sunset. Contentment is the successful choice of where to put attention.

As I sit here in my little studio writing, I can be aware of my writing deadline, and the course I am delivering this coming weekend and the million and one things that need to be done before school closes a mere two weeks away – Christmas presents and school plays and music concerts and birthday parties and gifts, and also the possibility of going away and the need to explore this – all of which spells stress, or ... I can look out of my window and celebrate the fact that I am here, opposite the harbour, in Cape Town, living by the sea as I always wanted to, being a writer like I wanted to. The sun is shining and I am healthy and well. I am in credit, and I have a healthy, loving family. All is well.

Being content is the realisation that everything is as it should be

Containment is a big topic, particularly in a world that celebrates consumerism – the very opposite of containment. We need to cultivate the ability to contain – our skills, dreams, aspirations; our joy, love, wealth; our relationships; our work; our spirituality; our lives.

The more we can contain, the more we become content, and the more life can flow. Mostly we keep looking at what is outside our container – that which we don't have, rather than embracing, holding, having and celebrating what we do have.

I meet many people in my practice who have so much, but cannot see it. Not just the non-tangible stuff like joy and freedom, but actual wealth too. They are too busy looking at what they don't have; they are too concerned with what their money can't buy. Without contentment and containment wealth not only becomes meaningless, it dissipates quickly too.

Being content is an act of opening your heart. And when you open you heart you usually want to share. So count your blessings and recognise where you are and how far you have come. Cultivate contentment and containment.

Beyond practising contentment, to contain wealth you need to explore containers – in other words, you need to become informed. Find out the various investment options available. Explore possibilities for business. Do your homework. Take the time to look at options in detail and at length. Do not jump into the first opportunity that comes your way if you have not looked at all your options. On the other hand, do not become immobilised by the many choices.

This is not the place to make changes – this is where you contain and explore your options for containment.

On Wealth Arrival – Be Content:

- What do I need to contain?
- What am I grateful for?
- How do I want to contain my wealth?
- Who can help me?
- How can I practise contentment?

These questions can be answered on many levels. The main thing to realise is that *you must practise containment and contentment.*

Realisation: *I have every reason to be content.*

Focus: Count your blessings, contain what you have, share

5. Fifth I – I am at the destination I have chosen – Fine-tuning

To properly contain your wealth, and to be content, you need to accept and acknowledge that this 'here' place where you are is the destination you have actually chosen, and then you need to fine-tune.

When you sell your business to pursue writing and teaching, or you leave your high-paying job because you want to travel using your inheritance money, or you take a retrenchment package because your job makes you miserable and you go off to find yourself on a stud farm – you may initially feel that you 'don't fit'. And initially you won't.

You may question, when it comes down to it, whether it is in fact writing, or travel or finding yourself that you are after. And when this happens you may try to find someone to blame for where you are in your life at the moment. Though part of you is relieved to be moving on, another part of you longs for the known and the familiar.

Also, under the glamorous sheen of distance, the past begins to take on a much rosier hue than reality ever offered. You may wonder why you left your business or job in the first place. You will certainly start to miss the perks. You will also miss being the old you. Until you have finalised your new direction, you will be unable to be either the old you, or the new, 'being formed' you. And in this process much fine-tuning will be required until you get it right, until you get the new 'you' right – in the right place, doing the right thing, doing the thing that fits.

Take up the reins – this is the destination you have chosen

Now most of us know that we need to be, do, have – in that order – but we also need to examine the equation the other way round. Sometimes what we have and what we do, does not fit who we are. And sometimes, in the act of creating a new beingness, we need to try on different suits of doing to see which fits us best. This is particularly the case if we are moving into a creative or artistic life, or the life of a teacher or healer.

For example, after I sold my business, I planned to 'uplift the world', through 'healing and teaching and writing'. I was not sure what form the 'healing, teaching and writing' would take, and it took nearly a decade to fine-tune by trying out various options and seeing how they fit. In between, I added training in a few more healing modalities, I trained as a writer, I delivered business coaching and strategising, I tweaked and fiddled, created and facilitated courses, then stopped so I could write. It took a long time. But while I was fine-tuning I was learning, trying out what works, testing to see what produces results, and integrating what I had learnt in the business world into my new life as teacher. I was finding out what it is I know and, eventually, how to deliver healing of a different kind. I was creating new processes, my processes, and developing transformational stuff that had never existed before.

Now, a decade later I can say 'yes, I am a teacher, writer and healer' but it's in a way I had definitely not imagined when I arrived here at 'Affluence'. What I am saying is, don't expect to have all the details filled in when you arrive at your wealth destination. Part of Living in Wealth is continuous fine-tuning.

Take up the reins and don't look back

You do have to remind yourself that this is what you chose – even when it looks dubious. You need to remember what you were trying to do, where you had planned to go when you set off on your Wealth Journey and then fine-tune the details through testing to see how things fit. You also need to remember to trust yourself.

If you succumb to looking at the past through rose-coloured glasses you will head straight back there pronto – and many do. People go off to live in another country and then return. Or they plan to become a writer their whole life and then don't get it together when it comes down to it.

When you arrive at your destination, remind yourself that 'this is where you were going', then fine-tune the details.

On Wealth Arrival – Fine-tune:

- What did I set out to do?
- Who did I set out to become?
- What draws me now?
- What can I practise that will bring me closer to my goal?
- What do I need to let go of?

These questions can be answered on many levels. The main thing to realise is that *you created this new reality.*

Realisation: *I am here because I chose this place – I can fine-tune it to fit me perfectly*

Focus: Purpose, trying to see what fits

6. Sixth I – I rejoice – Celebrate!!

When did you last REJOICE? Actually, fully, and totally REJOICE!

Rejoice means *Celebrate! Express Joy! Cheer! Exult! Delight!*

When did you last do that? And how many times in your life have you *ever* done that? Sad to say, I can count my rejoicing moments on my hands – both hands at a stretch – most of the real rejoicing on one hand only. Sad, isn't it?

But there have been periods of my life when I have been in that space for a few months at a time. Those were times when I had fallen in love, or was in the midst of spiritual revelation.

Rejoicing and celebrating do not have to be grand events; they are actually a state of mind. And the really useful thing about this is that it opens up the flows – of money, joy, wealth, all good things.

Rejoicing is not an outcome, it's a choice and a decision to live life in a certain way – no matter what external reality looks like. Very few people live this way, even when they have reason to celebrate. I see people in my practice daily, who have every possible reason to be rejoicing – good health, no entanglements, freedom, wealth, loving relationships, and yet, they are still not happy.

In fact I can go as far as to say that when it comes down to it, most people just want to be happy. They want to feel at peace. They want to be in a state of rejoicing. It's not really more money they are after, or a better job or house, or even a better husband or wife – just happiness.

When I ask people how they will know if their wealth alignment or money alchemy course 'worked' and what needs to happen in their lives for them to know the work is producing results, most reply something along the lines of 'feeling happier'. They want more contentment, more joy, peace, being on purpose. Only a tiny percentage mention an increase in cash or earnings and it's usually in addition to the feel-good feelings. People want to feel good. Period.

Celebrate! Express Joy! Cheer! Exult! Delight!

Now if we realise and truly embrace the fact that nothing that happens externally can actually add to our joy in the long run, and acknowledge that we are responsible for *cultivating* joy and a sense of rejoicing, then we leap frog ahead along our wealth path.

Rejoicing is a truly wonderful thing to do. And when we tune into rejoicing we realise there is so much to rejoice about. Rejoicing is also quite generative – the more you do it, the more it feeds on itself and grows.

Here is the tricky part, though, and it's also the secret of rejoicing itself. You need to start with rejoicing in yourself! If you think about it, it's logical. If you cannot rejoice in your own wondrousness, how will you do it about anyone or anything else? It is this that we have the most problems with.

We are not taught to value ourselves, nurture ourselves, rejoice in our achievements, love ourselves, pat ourselves on the back for a job well done. When last did you appreciate yourself? When last did you marvel at your body and the amazing work it does? When last did you pay tribute to your intuition, thanking it for the wonderful opportunities it leads you to? When last did you admire your admirable qualities? When last did you look in the mirror and say 'Girl (or Dude), you really rock!' – even (and especially) if you're sixty?

So, let's get that programme going, because if you can rejoice in yourself, what else do you need? It does not matter how you rejoice, what matters is that you do. Find your own little rituals that make you feel joyful and appreciated.

On Wealth Arrival – Rejoice!:

- Rejoice in your admirable qualities, talents and gifts
- Celebrate your health
- Admire your body
- Marvel at your endurance, fortitude and ability to survive
- Thank your intuition, instincts and mind for a great job
- Exult in your achievements
- Do a little dance of joy
- Deeply appreciate the Divine for everything you have
- Laugh at how easy it is to laugh
- Reflect on where you are and leap up with your arms in the air 8 times

- Say 'YAY!' till it feels like a celebration

Then do it all again! And then one more time! The main thing is to *REJOICE! REJOICE! REJOICE!*

Realisation: *I am here because I'm having fun!*

Focus: REJOICE! CELEBRATE! HAVE FUN!

7. Seventh I – I expand – New space

Now you are ready to take up your new space. Finally. And by now, you will have realised that this new space, here in the present, is not the same space as the space you once created from your past. In other words, not only do you need to take up the new wealthy space that you are in but you also have to expand it, to fit the actual picture that you are now living, and the new you that you are at the moment, which will be quite different from the you that you once aspired to become.

That's quite a mouthful, quite a thought, and quite a reality. You see once, way back then, from your 'then' perspective you created a future, a goal, a destination, and a new you. That, let's call it 'projection', was like a shadow casting forward from your 'then' reality. However, you have grown and changed and flourished and prospered along the way, so that by now that future reality in all probability no longer fits as well as it would have fitted five or ten or fifteen years ago when you created it.

You need to expand reality to fit the new you

So you need to update. You need to expand reality to fit you. You also need a new container that will have room for the new future you will have to start thinking about creating from here. For unless you expand you will contract. That is natural law. When we look at nature we find that it is ever abundant, ever expansive, and when that stops, decay and death follow. We are a part of nature and so the same is true for us.

What does it mean in reality to take up your new space? It means to step into the new shoes you have created. It is very much like stepping into a new position at work. For this new wealthy life is in fact a new position, and unless you take up your duties and start to perform them, you may find yourself demoted to the way things were before.

Taking up your new duties is, firstly, an attitude. Secondly, it's the development of new habits and ways of being. It's adopting new ways to look at the world, new belief systems. It's cultivating new routines. It's also taking on new responsibilities. When you lose weight, you need a new wardrobe of clothes. If you continue wearing your old clothes, you will soon grow back into your old body. It's the same with wealth.

Many people revert back to where they were with regard to wealth because they do not 'up their game'. Your new position in life means you need to reconfigure and take some new decisions. Where will you live? What will you do from here on? Who will you mix with? Where will you hang out? What will you believe? Who are you becoming?

Some of these decisions will not be easy. But unless you embrace the new you, and your new space, it will fade away like mist. It's like moving into a new, bigger house. Some of your furniture and blinds and curtains will fit, and some will have to be moved on. Now you have to make those decisions with your life. And a quick rule of thumb is to weigh everything up against the following questions:

- Does this person/belief/attitude/location/way of doing things/dress/pen *fit the new me?*
- Does this person/belief/attitude/location/way of doing things/dress/pen *belong to the present or the past?*
- Does this person/belief/attitude/location/way of doing things/dress/pen *add value to my life?*
- Is this person/belief/attitude/location/way of doing things/dress/pen *part of my new future?*
- Which version of me does this person/belief/attitude/location/way of doing things *reflect?*

Initially you may be minus a few drinking spots, or a few friends or a few ideas, but soon, very soon, the space you have created will become filled with brand new wondrousness of your choice – quite fabulous, very expansive, and in resonance with your new space. You need to surround yourself with things, people, ideas, beliefs and ways of doing and being, that add support to your new space and life.

On Wealth Arrival – Expand into your new space:

- Create 8 new beliefs about life that reflect where you are now
- Create 8 new ways of doing things that reflect where you are now
- Reflect on 3 new attitudes you need to cultivate
- Choose 3 new hobbies, 3 new friends and 3 new habits that reflect the new you
- Let go of anything that is not a part of the new space
- Adjust your wardrobe to reflect the new you that you are becoming
- Take 3 inspired decisions that will help you take up your new wealth space

The main thing is to *EXPAND into your new life*

Realisation: *The person who set the goal of where I am now all that time ago, is not the same person as the person who has arrived here. I am not the same person as the person who set this goal that I have now achieved*

Focus: Expand and adjust your goal to fit the current you

8. Eighth I – I dream – New reality

A few weeks ago, while giving a talk to promote my book *The Money Well,* which deals with containment, I was asked, 'What is *your* container'? It was not an easy question to answer. For although I said my books, and Wealth Works, my company which incorporates my work in writing and teaching and a few other things I have planned for the future, I have not really created a very clear container for the future.

That is one of the dangers in 'arriving' at your destination. You are now 'HERE'. And unless you have the benefit of this book ... or some very wise counsel ... your mind will say 'Game over. You won. End of chat.'

Alas, this can be a big problem. Not initially, but certainly over time. Now, this section, 'Living the 9 "I's" of wealth', deals with 'What to do once you get there', 'there' being wealth, and in so doing is concerned with accepting and having and being this new wealthy you, in this new wealth space. However, once you have embraced that, you need to look at creating a new future beyond this point.

What is interesting about creating from this space is that most of what you will now want may not be physical. This is probably the biggest impediment to moving forward once you 'arrive'– the thought or feeling that you have everything you need, which you most probably do. However, unless you move forward you will die – if not physically and literally then out of boredom, restlessness and discontent.

Once you have everything, you come to understand that having everything is not enough, and it may never have been what you wanted in the first place. You start to question your life, your work, and your relationships. You may start to question your purpose and your future.

You need to move forward. You need to keep going

This is a truly wonderful place to be, and the sooner you get to this point of questioning, the better. Because once you have got there and come to these realisations, then you can begin to create some truly spectacular things. And these truly spectacular things, if you are reading this book, will probably have something to do with the world beyond your needs. It will also have to do with going after what you truly want, living the life you really want to live – which very often may not be what you just spent twenty years creating. So the sooner you get 'there' or rather 'here', the better.

The eighth 'I' can also be a very hard place to be because you may need to make some difficult choices. By now you have a good grip on the creation process, you know you can have what you want, and you are faced with the frightening prospect of deciding exactly what that is. It is also exciting because you can bring out all those old dreams and aspirations that you may have parked along the way.

The key thing is to create some new dreams. Create a new reality to move towards, and this time, do it for the betterment of all mankind (that's an optional extra, anyway ...)

On Wealth Arrival – Create a new dream:

- Reflect and list old dreams and aspirations. Do any still draw you?
- Write a list of possible careers, things you could do/ become
- Consider how you could help uplift the world
- Create a vision for the next decade (no matter how old you are)
- Connect with your purpose through prayer, reflection and meditation

The main thing is to *CREATE a new dream for your life*

Realisation: *I can dream for the world*

Focus: On how you can help and serve the greater whole

9. Ninth I – I AM – Be!

I have just delivered a Money Well™ course this past weekend. It is a general trend for people to come out of my courses feeling connected with their own power. In addition to feeling empowered, however, the course participants this last weekend really got an 'aha!', moment out of my reminding them that they are enough.

The subject of the course was containment of wealth and expansion of wealth. Expansion of wealth is a reflection of expansion of self. The subject of containment begins with the need for a container. We need to create one. We need to have one. Our container is our goal and destination and quest for a new self. Because what we are really trying to contain is ourselves.

We are trying to contain our own magnificence, for we are all truly magnificent and awesome beings. We are all perfect, and complete. Even as we try to transform, what we are really trying to do is recognise our own divinity and perfection. It is good to remember this, in our quest for transformation. We need to be clear that what we are really trying to transform is our illusion. We are trying to take away the blinkers that we wear that tell us that we are not enough – not good enough, not smart enough, not attractive enough, not masculine enough, not feminine enough, not wealthy enough, not enough.

We are trying to contain our own magnificence!

Our journey is really a journey of acceptance of self – the light as well as the shadow. We come to our journey to recognise that we are the light and the shadow intertwined. We come to our journey to learn to love and accept both.

It is not that we have to take this horrid, incomplete, flawed, non-creative self and mould it into something else. It's not that we have to somehow reconfigure ourselves into something better. It's not that now that we have all these coaches and trainers and transformational people around we can change our undesirable selves into more desirable ones, like some kind of spiritual or personality face lift.

Let's face it, most of the world believes in one or other kind of Divine, omnipotent and awesome Creator – we call that Divine energy God, Allah, Jehovah, Krishna. We believe that this is an energy of perfection of which we are a part. Therefore how can we believe that that perfect and divine energy would create anything that is other than perfect and divine?

Yes, there has been some miscommunication, misrepresentation, and therefore confusion about the way things really are, about the way we truly are. But we can let that story go.

Embrace your Divinity right now. Come to the recognition that you are superb! You are fantastic! You are awesome! You are quirky and angry and whingey and talented and a real cow around the full moon (is that what they mean by 'the cow jumped over the moon'?). Realise, right now, that you have everything you need inside of you. Where else would it be? Who knows you better than yourself? Who can advise you better than you can? Who knows better what is good for you and what you should avoid?

Arise, and take up your power! Stop pretending. Stop listening to old tales of who you are. Stop believing your story.

Be. Be here. Be alive. Be present. Be yourself. Be happy. Be creative. Be sad. Be angry. Be well. Be foolish. Be sloppy. Be Divine. Be joyful. Be humorous. Be absurd. Be whatever you want to be. Be now. Be tomorrow. Be wealthy. Become.

Arise, and take up your power!

Being is what we all yearn for. The contentment in recognising that we are, and we are enough. It is only once you know that you are enough, that you become truly wealthy. And until you really know that, no amount of wealth will ever be enough.

On Wealth Arrival – Be!:

- Reflect on your magnificence and uniqueness
- Write a list of all your virtues, talents and gifts
- Reflect upon and embrace your 'vices' – lightly and humorously

- Stare into your eyes in the mirror and say 'I love you'
- Connect with the core of Divinity within
- Consider that there is only one of you on the planet! Wow!

The main thing is to *BE!*

Realisation: *I Am, and I am enough.*

Focus: On the fact that you are completely and totally unique

Wrapping it all up in a Golden Weave

This section has dealt with the process of accepting and becoming the new wealthy you once you arrive at your destination. This destination is the place we arrive at when any goal is achieved – big or small. It could be when you arrive at a new job, or once you have navigated one of the Wealth Consciousness levels. It could be when you overcome an addiction to cigarettes, or once you have expanded into having a new branch in your business.

Go through the process of arriving and integrating your new space and being. It will help you to contain, absorb and move forward.

Like everything in this book, go through the steps lightly and with intent. You can also use these nine steps for trouble-shooting if you become stuck once you have 'arrived'.

Don't get stuck in the arrivals lounge – even if it's the business class or first class lounge. Life must continue, and the Wealth Journey never ends.

About the Author

Kiki Theo is a writer, transformational facilitator, healer, wife and mother. After successfully selling her fund management business, she retired from the business world to fulfil her dream to write and teach about holistic wealth creation. By combining three decades of business experience with her lifelong study and practice of metaphysics, she has created a truly unique approach to money making which aims to create Wealth-Being™. Kiki is the creator of *Money Well*™ *& Money Alchemy*™ transformational processing and the originator of the *Wealth Journey*™ wealth consciousness model. She is a full-time writer and teacher with an extensive seminar schedule.

Kiki lives in Cape Town with her husband, two young children, and a black cat called Marzipan.

She writes in her little studio overlooking the harbour and is currently busy with her next book, *Relationship Alchemy*® ~ *Money & Relationship*.

For more details about the author and her work see www.moneyalchemy.com

The next book!
RELATIONSHIP ALCHEMY® ~ Money & Relationship

Money is something you are in relationship with. It reflects other relationships in your life. Everything is connected. In **Relationship Alchemy®** we take a close look at the various archetypal energies that flow through us and that we connect with in our primary and most significant relationships.

We will look at the way we relate to these energies both internally and in the world around us. We will reflect on our historic relationships as well as on the imprints that these have left in our psyches, attitude and belief systems, with special reference to wealth and its creation.

Focusing on the archetypes of Mother, Father, Child, and Lover we will examine the interplay of these energies in our life and work, and discover their effect on the creation of wealth. Using a variety of original processes, we will move towards understanding and balancing the masculine (positive, yang, active) and feminine (negative, yin, passive) energies in our relationship with money, self and others, thereby opening up and aligning our wealth flow.

Clearing and rebalancing your core relationships across time will release additional energy and focus; add power, strength and direction; and activate money flow. When you clarify your relationship with money, align it with clear purpose and intent, it will flow ... like magic.

Using Kiki's latest *Relationship Revitalising*™ *Process,* contained in this book, you can create a vibrant new energetic template to attract and maintain healthy, happy relationship with wealth, self, and others. *Relationship Alchemy®* is a powerful, light, magical book that will give you wings!

Acknowledgements

I would like to thank all the *Money Alchemists* who attend my courses and wealth alignments for helping me shape my work (and self) with their presence and willingness. I thank them for allowing me to guide their journey of transformation with such total confidence and trust. I thank them especially for their skilful use of this material which creates such fabulous results and helps the work (and me) to shine as a result – you make it happen! I also thank the readers of my books for their warm, generous and inspiring feedback. It is always such a pleasure to hear from you. You are all my teachers.

A special and warm thank you to everyone at Penguin for continuing to support me on my journey to becoming an internationally best-selling author! Thank you, Maire, for your always fabulous editing. (Please don't edit this sentence . . .)

I am grateful to all my wonderful friends for their love and support and especially to Simone and Craig for sharing so much fun and laughter with me. Thank you especially to Linda Hawkins, the godmother of these books, for spreading the word on this work around the world with gold and glitter!

And, lastly, thank you to my family – my husband Shaun and children Alex and Sasha – for allowing me the time and space for this work and for helping me transform into a real human being. I love you.